Fortinet
SD-WAN

Administration Guide

7.2.0

NSE4

NSE5

NSE6

NSE7

Jhason Berrison

Table of Contents

SD-WAN overview

SD-WAN is a software-defined approach to managing Wide-Area Networks (WAN). It consolidates the physical transport connections, or underlays, and monitors and load-balances traffic across the links. VPN overlay networks can be built on top of the underlays to control traffic across different sites.

Health checks and SD-WAN rules define the expected performance and business priorities, allowing the FortiGate to automatically and intelligently route traffic based on the application, internet service, or health of a particular connection.

WAN security and intelligence can be extended into the LAN by incorporating wired and wireless networks under the same domain. FortiSwitch and FortiAP devices integrate seamlessly with the FortiGate to form the foundation of an SD-Branch.

Some of the key benefits of SD-WAN include:

- Reduced cost with transport independence across MPLS, 4G/5G LTE, and others.
- Reduced complexity with a single vendor and single-pane-of-glass management.
- Improve business application performance thanks to increased availability and agility.
- Optimized user experience and efficiency with SaaS and public cloud applications.

SD-WAN components

SD-WAN can be broken down into three layers:

- Management and orchestration
- Control, data plane, and security
- Network access

The control, data plane, and security layer can only be deployed on a FortiGate. The other two layers can help to scale and enhance the solution. For large deployments, FortiManager and FortiAnalyzer provide the management and orchestration capabilities FortiSwitch and FortiAP provide the components to deploy an SD-Branch.

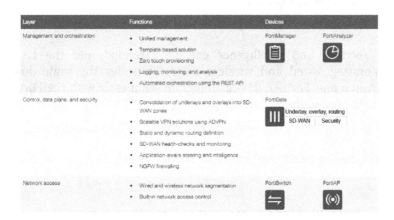

Layer	Functions	Devices	
Management and orchestration	• Unified management • Template based solution • Zero touch provisioning • Logging, monitoring, and analysis • Automated orchestration using the REST API	FortiManager	FortiAnalyzer
Control, data plane, and security	• Consolidation of underlays and overlays into SD-WAN zones • Scalable VPN solutions using ADVPN • Static and dynamic routing definition • SD-WAN health-checks and monitoring • Application-aware steering and intelligence • NGFW firewalling	FortiGate Underlay, overlay, routing SD-WAN / Security	
Network access	• Wired and wireless network segmentation • Built-in network access control	FortiSwitch	FortiAP

SD-WAN designs and architectures

The core functionalities of Fortinet's SD-WAN solution are built into the FortiGate. Whether the environment contains one FortiGate, or one hundred, you can use SD-WAN by enabling it on the individual FortiGates.

At a basic level, SD-WAN can be deployed on a single device in a single site environment:

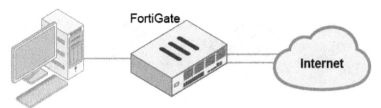

At a more advanced level, SD-WAN can be deployed in a multi-site, hub and spoke environment:

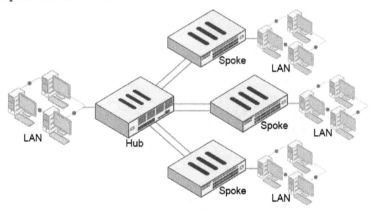

At an enterprise or MSSP level, the network can include multiple hubs, possibly across multiple regions:

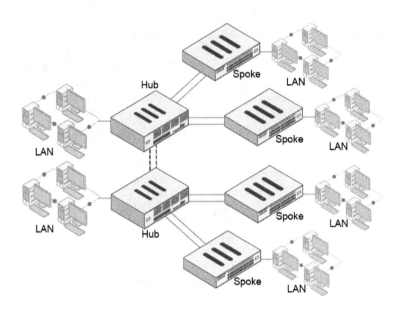

SD-WAN designs principles

The Five-pillar approach, described in the SD-WAN / SD-Branch Architecture for MSSPs guide, is recommended when designing a secure SD-WAN solution.

Pillar	Overview
Underlay	Choose the WAN links to use.
Overlay	Choose the topology to interconnect your sites.
Routing	Choose how to propagate routes between your sites.
Security	Choose how to protect each of the available paths.
SD-WAN	Choose the strategy used to pick one of the available paths.

Underlay

Determine the WAN links that will be used for the underlay network, such as your broadband link, MPLS, 4G/5G LTE connection, and others.

For each link, determine the bandwidth, quality and reliability (packet loss, latency, and jitter), and cost. Use this information to determine which link to prefer, what type of traffic to send across the each link, and to help you the baselines for health-checks.

Overlay

VPN overlays are needed when traffic must travel across multiple sites. These are usually site-to-site IPsec tunnels that interconnect branches, datacenters, and the cloud, forming a hub-and-spoke topology.

The management and maintenance of the tunnels should be considered when determining the overlay network requirements. Manual tunnel configuration might be sufficient in a small environment, but could become unmanageable as the environment size increases. ADVPN can be used to help scale the solution.

Routing

Traditional routing designs manipulate routes to steer traffic to different links. SD-WAN uses traditional routing to build the basic routing table to reach different destinations, but uses SD-WAN rules to steer traffic. This allows the steering to be based on criteria such as destination, internet service, application, route tag, and the health of the link. Routing in an

SD-WAN solution is used to identify all possible routes across the underlays and overlays, which the FortiGate balances using ECMP.

In the most basic configuration, static gateways that are configured on an SD-WAN member interface automatically provide the basic routing needed for the FortiGate to balance traffic across the links. As the number of sites and destinations increases, manually maintaining routes to each destination becomes difficult. Using dynamic routing to advertise routes across overlay tunnels should be considered when you have many sites to interconnect.

Security

Security involves defining policies for access control and applying the appropriate protection using the FortiGate's NGFW features. Efficiently grouping SD-WAN members into SD-WAN zones must also be considered. Typically, underlays provide direct internet access and overlays provide remote internet or network access. Grouping the underlays together into one zone, and the overlays into one or more zones could be an effective method.

SD-WAN

The SD-WAN pillar is the intelligence that is applied to traffic steering decisions. It is comprised of four primary elements:

- **SD-WAN zones**

  SD-WAN is divided into zones. SD-WAN member interfaces are assigned to zones, and zones are used in policies as source and destination interfaces. You can define multiple zones to group SD-WAN interfaces together, allowing logical groupings for overlay and underlay interfaces. Routing can be configured per zone.

- **SD-WAN members**

  Also called interfaces, SD-WAN members are the ports and interfaces that are used to run traffic. At least one interface must be configured for SD-WAN to function.

- **Performance SLAs**

  Also called health-checks, performance SLAs are used to monitor member interface link quality, and to detect link failures. When the SLA falls below a configured threshold, the route can be removed, and traffic can be steered to different links in the SD-WAN rule.

6

SLA health-checks use active or passive probing:

- Active probing requires manually defining the server to be probed, and generates consistent probing traffic.

- Passive probing uses active sessions that are passing through firewall policies used by the related SD-WAN interfaces to derive health measurements. It reduces the amount of configuration, and eliminates probing traffic. See Passive WAN health measurement for details.

- **SD-WAN rules**

  Also called services, SD-WAN rules control path selection. Specific traffic can be dynamically sent to the best link, or use a specific route

  Rules control the strategy that the FortiGate uses when selecting the outbound traffic interface, the SLAs that are monitored when selecting the outgoing interface, and the criteria for selecting the traffic that adheres to the rule. When no SD-WAN rules match the traffic, the implicit rule applies.

SD-WAN quick start

This section provides an example of how to start using SD-WAN for load balancing and redundancy.

In this example, two ISP internet connections, wan1 (DHCP) and wan2 (static), use SD-WAN to balance traffic between them at 50% each.

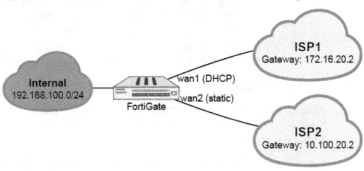

1. Configuring the SD-WAN interface

2. Adding a static route

3. Selecting the implicit SD-WAN algorithm

4. Configuring firewall policies for SD-WAN

5. Link monitoring and failover

6. Results

7. Configuring SD-WAN in the CLI

Configuring the SD-WAN interface

First, SD-WAN must be enabled and member interfaces must be selected and added to a zone. The selected FortiGate interfaces can be of any type (physical, aggregate, VLAN, IPsec, and others), but must be removed from any other configurations on the FortiGate.

In this step, two interfaces are configured and added to the default SD-WAN zone (virtual-wan-link) as SD-WAN member interfaces. This example uses a mix of static and dynamic IP addresses; your deployment could also use only one or the other.

Once the SD-WAN members are created and added to a zone, the zone can be used in firewall policies, and the whole SD-WAN can be used in static routes.

To configure SD-WAN members:

1. Configure the wan1 and wan2 interfaces. Set the wan1 interface Addressing mode to DHCP and Distance to 10. By default, a DHCP interface has a distance of 5, and a static route has a distance of 10. It is important to account for this when configuring your SD-WAN for 50/50 load balancing by setting the DHCP interface's distance to 10

2. Set the wan2 interface IP/Netmask to 10.100.20.1 255.255.255.0.

2. Go to Network > SD-WAN, select the SD-WAN Zones tab, and click Create New > SD-WAN Member.

3. Set the Interface to wan1.

4. Leave SD-WAN Zone as virtual-wan-link.

5. As wan1 uses DHCP, leave Gateway set to 0.0.0.0.

   If IPv6 visibility is enabled in the GUI, an IPv6 gateway can also be added for each member.

6. Leave Cost as 0.

   The Cost field is used by the Lowest Cost (SLA) strategy. The link with the lowest cost is chosen to pass traffic. The lowest possible Cost is 0.

7. Set Status to Enable, and click OK.

8. Repeat the above steps for wan2, setting Gateway to the ISP's gateway: 10.100.20.2.

Adding a static route

You must configure a default route for the SD-WAN. The default gateways for each SD-WAN member interface do not need to be defined in the static routes table. FortiGate will decide what route or routes are preferred using Equal Cost Multi-Path (ECMP) based on distance and priority.

To create a static route for SD-WAN:

1. Go to Network > Static Routes.

2. Click Create New. The New Static Route page opens.

3. Set Destination to Subnet, and leave the IP address and subnet mask as 0.0.0.0/0.0.0.0.

4. In the Interface field select an SD-WAN zone.

5. Ensure that Status is Enabled.

6. Click OK.

Selecting the implicit SD-WAN algorithm

SD-WAN rules define specific routing options to route traffic to an SD-WAN member.

If no routing rules are defined, the default Implicit rule is used. It can be configured to use one of five different load balancing algorithms.

This example shows four methods to equally balance traffic between the two WAN connections. Go to Network > SD-WAN, select the SD-WAN Rules tab, and edit the sd-wan rule to select the method that is appropriate for your requirements.

- Source IP (CLI command: source-ip-based):

    Select this option to balance traffic equally between the SD-WAN members according to a hash algorithm based on the source IP addresses.

- Session (weight-based):

    Select this option to balance traffic equally between the SD-WAN members by the session numbers ratio among its members. Use weight 50 for each of the 2 members.

- Source-Destination IP (source-dest-ip-based):

    Select this option to balance traffic equally between the SD-WAN members according to a hash algorithm based on the source and destination IP addresses.

- Volume (measured-volume-based):

    Select this option to balance traffic equally between the SD-WAN members according to the bandwidth ratio among its members.

Configuring firewall policies for SD-WAN

SD-WAN zones can be used in policies as source and destination interfaces. Individual SD-WAN members cannot be used in policies.

You must configure a policy that allows traffic from your organization's internal network to the SD-WAN zone. Policies configured with the SD-WAN zone apply to all SD-WAN interface members in that zone.

To create a firewall policy for SD-WAN:

1. Go to Policy & Objects > Firewall Policy.

2. Click Create New. The New Policy page opens.

3. Configure the following:

Name	Enter a name for the policy.
Incoming Interface	internal
Outgoing Interface	virtual-wan-link
Source	all
Destination	all
Schedule	always
Service	ALL
Action	ACCEPT
Firewall / Network Options	Enable NAT and set IP Pool Configuration to Use Outgoing Interface Address.
Security Profiles	Apply profiles as required.
Logging Options	Enable Log Allowed Traffic and select All Sessions. This allows you to verify results later.

4. Enable the policy, then click OK.

Link monitoring and failover

Performance SLA link monitoring measures the health of links that are connected to SD-WAN member interfaces by sending probing signals through each link to a server, and then measuring the link quality based on latency, jitter, and packet loss. If a link is broken, the routes on that link are removed and traffic is routed through other links. When the link is working again, the routes are re-enabled. This prevents traffic being sent to a broken link and lost.

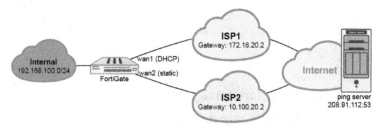

In this example, the detection server IP address is 208.91.112.53. A performance SLA is created so that, if ping fails per the metrics defined, the routes to that interface are removed and traffic is detoured to the other interface. The ping protocol is used, but other protocols could also be selected as required.

To configure a performance SLA:

1. Go to Network > SD-WAN, select the Performance SLAs tab, and click Create New.

2. Enter a name for the SLA and set Protocol to Ping.

3. In the Server field, enter the detection server IP address (208.91.112.53 in this example).

4. In the Participants field, select Specify and add wan1 and wan2.

SLA targets are not required for link monitoring.

5. Configure the required metrics in Link Status.

6. Ensure that Update static route is enabled. This disables static routes for the inactive interface and restores routes on recovery.

7. Click OK.

Results

The following GUI pages show the function of the SD-WAN and can be used to confirm that it is setup and running correctly:

- Interface usage
- Performance SLA
- Routing table
- Firewall policy

Interface usage

Go to Network > SD-WAN and select the SD-WAN Zones tab to review the SD-WAN interfaces' usage.

Bandwidth

Select Bandwidth to view the amount of downloaded and uploaded data for each interface.

Volume

Select Volume to see donut charts of the received and sent bytes on the interfaces.

Sessions

Select Sessions to see a donut chart of the number of active sessions on each interface.

Performance SLA

Go to Network > SD-WAN, select the Performance SLAs tab, and select the SLA from the table (server in this example) to view the packet loss, latency, and jitter on each SD-WAN member in the health check server.

Packet loss

Select Packet Loss to see the percentage of packets lost for each member.

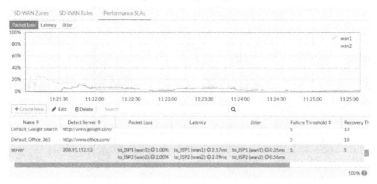

Latency

Select Latency to see the current latency, in milliseconds, for each member.

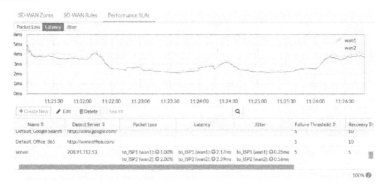

Jitter

Select Jitter to see the jitter, in milliseconds, for each member.

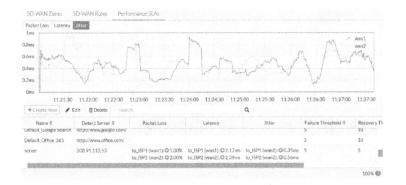

Routing table

Go to Dashboard > Network, expand the Routing widget, and select Static & Dynamic to review all static and dynamic routes.

Firewall policy

Go to Policy & Objects > Firewall Policy to review the SD-WAN policy.

Configuring SD-WAN in the CLI

This example can be entirely configured using the CLI.

To configure SD-WAN in the CLI:

1. Configure the wan1 and wan2 interfaces:

```
config system interface
    edit "wan1"
        set alias to_ISP1
        set mode dhcp
        set distance 10
    next
    edit "wan2"
        set alias to_ISP2
        set ip 10.100.20.1 255.255.255.0
    next
end
```

2. Enable SD-WAN and add the interfaces as members:

```
config system sdwan
    set status enable
    config members
        edit 1
            set interface "wan1"
        next
        edit 2
            set interface "wan2"
            set gateway 10.100.20.2
        next
    end
```

end

3. Create a static route for SD-WAN:

```
config router static
    edit 1
        set sdwan-zone "virtual-wan-link"
    next
end
```

4. Select the implicit SD-WAN algorithm:

```
config system sdwan
        set load-balance-mode {source-ip-based | weight-
        based | source-dest-ip-based | measured-volume-
        based}
        end
```

5. Create a firewall policy for SD-WAN:

```
config firewall policy
    edit <policy_id>
        set name <policy_name>
        set srcintf "internal"
        set dstintf "virtual-wan-link"
        set srcaddr all
        set dstaddr all
        set action accept
        set schedule always
        set service ALL
        set utm-status enable
        set ssl-ssh-profile <profile_name>
        set av-profile <profile_name>
```

```
                    set webfilter-profile <profile_name>
                    set dnsfilter-profile <profile_name>
                    set emailfilter-profile <profile_name>
                    set ips_sensor <sensor_name>
                    set application-list <app_list>
                    set voip-profile <profile_name>
                    set logtraffic all
                    set nat enable
                    set status enable
                next
            end
```

6.   Configure a performance SLA:

```
            config system sdwan
                config health-check
                    edit "server"
                        set server "208.91.112.53"
                        set update-static-route enable
                        set members 1 2
                    next
                end
            end
```

Results

To view the routing table:

get router info routing-table all

Routing table for VRF=0

Codes: K - kernel, C - connected, S - static, R - RIP, B - BGP

    O - OSPF, IA - OSPF inter area

N1 - OSPF NSSA external type 1, N2 - OSPF NSSA external type 2

E1 - OSPF external type 1, E2 - OSPF external type 2

i - IS-IS, L1 - IS-IS level-1, L2 - IS-IS level-2, ia - IS-IS inter area

* - candidate default

S*   0.0.0.0/0 [1/0] via 172.16.20.2, wan1

          [1/0] via 10.100.20.2, wan2

C   10.100.20.0/24 is directly connected, wan2

C   172.16.20.2/24 is directly connected, wan1

C   192.168.0.0/24 is directly connected, internal

To diagnose the Performance SLA status:

FGT # **diagnose sys sdwan health-check**

Health Check(server):

Seq(1): state(alive), packet-loss(0.000%) latency(15.247), jitter(5.231) sla_map=0x0

Seq(2): state(alive), packet-loss(0.000%) latency(13.621), jitter(6.905) sla_map=0x0

SD-WAN zones

SD-WAN is divided into zones. SD-WAN member interfaces are assigned to zones, and zones are used in policies, static routes, and SD-WAN rules.

You can define multiple zones to group SD-WAN interfaces together, allowing logical groupings for overlay and underlay interfaces. Zones are used in firewall policies, as source and destination interfaces, to allow for more granular control. SD-WAN members cannot be used directly in policies.

SD-WAN zones and members can both be used in IPv4 and IPv6 static routes to make route configuration more flexible, and in SD-WAN rules to simplify the rule configuration.

In the CLI:

- config system sdwan has replaced config system virtual-wan-link.

- diagnose sys sdwan has replaced diagnose sys virtual-wan-link.

- When configuring a static route, the sdwan-zone variable has replaced the sdwan variable.

When the Security Fabric is configured, SD-WAN zones are included in the Security Fabric topology views.

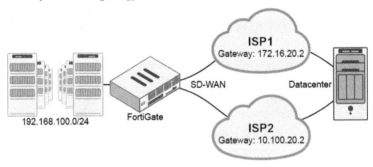

To create an SD-WAN zone in the GUI:

1. Go to Network > SD-WAN and select the SD-WAN Zones tab.

   The default SD-WAN zones are virtual-wan-link and SASE.

2. Click Create New > SD-WAN Zone.

3. Enter a name for the new zone, such as vpn-zone.

4. If SD-WAN members have already been created, add the required members to the zone.

   Members can also be added to the zone after it has been created by editing the zone, or when creating or editing the member.

5. Click OK.

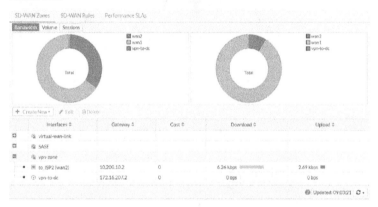

To create an SD-WAN interface member in the GUI:

1. Go to Network > SD-WAN, select the SD-WAN Zones tab, and click Create New > SD-WAN Member.

2. Select an interface.

   The interface can also be left as none and selected later, or click +VPN to create an IPsec VPN for the SD-WAN member.

3. Select the SD-WAN zone that the member will join. A member can also be moved to a different zone at any time.

4. Set the Gateway, Cost, and Status as required.

5. Click OK.

   The interface list at Network > Interfaces shows the SD-WAN zones and their members.

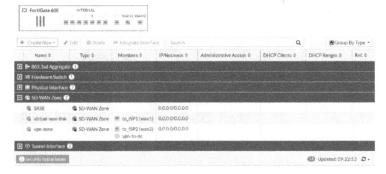

To create a policy using the SD-WAN zone in the GUI:

1. Go to Policy & Objects > Firewall Policy, Policy & Objects > Proxy Policy, or Policy & Objects > Security Policy.

2. Click Create New .

3. Configure the policy settings as needed, selecting an SD-WAN zone or zones for the incoming and/or outgoing interface.

4. Click OK.

To view SD-WAN zones in a Security Fabric topology:

1. Go to Security Fabric > Physical Topology or Security Fabric > Logical Topology. The SD-WAN zones and their members are shown.

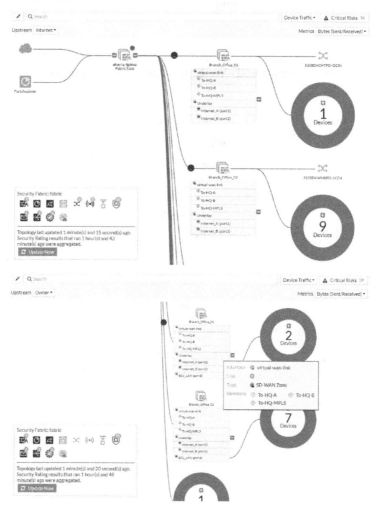

To configure SD-WAN in the CLI:

1. Enable SD-WAN and create a zone:

```
config system sdwan
    set status enable
    config zone
        edit "vpn-zone"
        next
    end
end
```

2. Configure SD-WAN members and add them to a zone:

```
config system sdwan
    config members
        edit 1
            set interface "to_ISP2"
            set zone "vpn-zone"
        next
        edit 2
            set interface "vpn-to-dc"
            set zone "vpn-zone"
        next
    end
end
```

To create a policy using the SD-WAN zone in the CLI:

```
config firewall policy
        edit 1
                set name sd-wan-1
                set srcintf internal
                set dstintf vpn-zone
                set srcaddr all
                set dstaddr all
                set action accept
                set schedule always
                set service ALL
                set utm-status enable
                set logtraffic all
                set nat enable
                set status enable
        next
    end
```

Specify an SD-WAN zone in static routes and SD-WAN rules

SD-WAN zones can be used in IPv4 and IPv6 static routes, and in SD-WAN service rules. This makes route configuration more flexible, and simplifies SD-WAN rule configuration.

To configure an SD-WAN zone in a static route in the GUI:

1. Go to Network > Static Routes

2. Edit an existing static route, or click Create New to create a new route.

3. Set Interface to one or more SD-WAN zones.

4. Configure the remaining settings are required.

5. Click OK.

To configure an SD-WAN zone in a static route in the CLI:

```
config router {static | static6}
    edit 1
        set sdwan-zone <zone> <zone> ...
    next
end
```

To configure an SD-WAN zone in an SD-WAN rule in the GUI:

1. Go to Network > SD-WAN and select the SD-WAN Rules tab

2. Edit an existing rule, or click Create New to create a new rule.

3. In the Zone preference field add one or more SD-WAN zones.

4. Configure the remaining settings are needed.

5. Click OK.

To configure an SD-WAN zone in an SD-WAN rule in the CLI:

```
config system sdwan
    config service
        edit 1
            set priority-zone <zone>
        next
    end
end
```

Examples

In these two examples, three SD-WAN members are created. Two members, port13 and port15, are in the default zone (virtual-wan-link), and the third member, to_FG_B_root, is in the SASE zone.

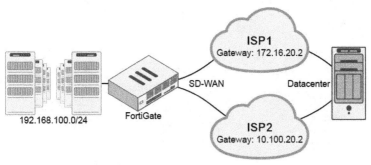

Example 1

In this example:

31

- Two service rules are created. Rule 1 uses the virtual-wan-link zone, and rule 2 uses the SASE zone.

- Two IPv4 static routes are created. The first route uses the virtual-wan-link zone, and the second route uses the SASE zone.

To configure the SD-WAN:

1. Assign port13 and port15 to the virtual-wan-link zone and to_FG_B_root to the SASE zone:

```
config system sdwan
    set status enable
    config members
        edit 1
            set interface "port13"
            set zone "virtual-wan-link"
            set gateway 10.100.1.1
        next
        edit 2
            set interface "port15"
            set zone "virtual-wan-link"
            set gateway 10.100.1.5
        next
        edit 3
            set interface "to_FG_B_root"
            set zone "SASE"
        next
    end
end
```

2. Create two service rules, one for each SD-WAN zone:

```
config system sdwan
    config service
        edit 1
            set dst "10.100.20.0"
            set priority-zone "virtual-wan-link"
        next
        edit 2
            set internet-service enable
            set internet-service-name "Fortinet-FortiGuard"
            set priority-zone "SASE"
        next
    end
end
```

3. Configure static routes for each of the SD-WAN zones:

```
config router static
    edit 1
        set distance 1
        set sdwan-zone "virtual-wan-link"
    next
    edit 2
        set dst 172.16.109.0 255.255.255.0
        set distance 1
        set sdwan-zone "SASE"
    next
end
```

To verify the results:

1. Check the service rule 1 diagnostics:

```
# diagnose sys sdwan service 1
```

Service(1): Address Mode(IPV4) flags=0x200 use-shortcut-sla

Gen(1),   TOS(0x0/0x0),   Protocol(0:   1->65535),
Mode(manual)

Members(2):

   1: Seq_num(1 port13), alive, selected

   2: Seq_num(2 port15), alive, selected

Dst address(1):

   10.100.20.0-10.100.20.255

Both members of the virtual-wan-link zone are selected. In
manual mode, the interface members are selected based
on the member configuration order. In SLA and priority
mode, the order depends on the link status. If all of the
link statuses pass, then the members are selected based on
the member configuration order.

2. Check the service rule 2 diagnostics:

```
# diagnose sys sdwan service 2
```

Service(2): Address Mode(IPV4) flags=0x200 use-shortcut-sla

Gen(1),   TOS(0x0/0x0),   Protocol(0:   1->65535),
Mode(manual)

Members(1):

   1: Seq_num(3 to_FG_B_root), alive, selected

      Internet   Service(1):   Fortinet-
      FortiGuard(1245324,0,0,0)

   The member of the SASE zone is selected.

3. Review the routing table:

```
# get router info routing-table static
```

Routing table for VRF=0

S*   0.0.0.0/0 [1/0] via 10.100.1.1, port13

[1/0] via 10.100.1.5, port15

        S   172.16.109.0/24 [1/0] via 172.16.206.2, to_FG_B_root

The default gateway has the members from the virtual-wan-link zone, and the route to 172.16.10.9.0/24 has the single member from the SASE zone.

Example 2

In this example, two IPv6 static routes are created. The first route uses the virtual-wan-link zone, and the second route uses the SASE zone.

To configure the SD-WAN:

Configure port13 and port15 with IPv6 addresses and assign them to the virtual-wan-link zone, and assign to_FG_B_root to the SASE zone:

```
config system sdwan
    set status enable
    config members
    edit 1
        set interface "port13"
        set zone "virtual-wan-link"
        set gateway6 2004:10:100:1::1
        set source6 2004:10:100:1::2
    next
    edit 2
        set interface "port15"
        set zone "virtual-wan-link"
        set gateway6 2004:10:100:1::5
        set source6 2004:10:100:1::6
    next
    edit 3
```

```
            set interface "to_FG_B_root"
            set zone "SASE"
        next
    end
end
```

Configure IPv6 static routes for each of the SD-WAN zones:

```
config router static6
    edit 1
        set distance 1
        set sdwan-zone "virtual-wan-link"
    next
    edit 2
        set dst 2003:172:16:109::/64
        set distance 1
        set sdwan-zone "SASE"
    next
            end
```

To verify the results:

Review the routing table:

```
# get router info6 routing-table static
Routing table for VRF=0
S*    ::/0 [1/0] via 2004:10:100:1::1, port13, 00:20:51, [1024/0]
          [1/0] via 2004:10:100:1::5, port15, 00:20:51, [1024/0]
S     2003:172:16:109::/64 [1/0] via ::ac10:ce02, to_FG_B_root,
00:20:51, [1024/0]
```

S   2003:172:16:209::/64 [5/0] via
::ac10:ce02, to_FG_B_root, 14:40:14, [1024/0]

The IPv6 default route includes the members from the virtual-wan-link zone, and the route to 2003:172:16:109::/64 has the single member from the SASE zone.

Performance SLA

The following topics provide instructions on configuring performance SLA:

- Link health monitor
- Factory default health checks
- Health check options
- Link monitoring example
- SLA targets example
- Passive WAN health measurement
- Passive health-check measurement by internet service and application
- Health check packet DSCP marker support
- Manual interface speedtest
- Scheduled interface speedtest
- Monitor performance SLA
- SLA monitoring using the REST API
- Mean opinion score calculation and logging in performance SLA health checks

Link health monitor

Performance SLA link health monitoring measures the health of links that are connected to SD-WAN member interfaces by either sending probing signals through each link to a server, or using session information that is captured on firewall policies, and measuring the link quality based on latency, jitter, and packet loss. If a link fails all of the health checks, the routes on that link are removed from the SD-WAN link load balancing group, and traffic is routed through other links. When the link is working again the routes are reestablished. This prevents traffic being sent to a broken link and lost.

When an SD-WAN member has multiple health checks configured, all of the checks must fail for the routes on that link to be removed from the SD-WAN link load balancing group.

Two health check servers can be configured to ensure that, if there is a connectivity issue, the interface is at fault and not the server. A server can only be used in one health check.

The FortiGate uses the first server configured in the health check server list to perform the health check. If the first server is unavailable, then the second server is used. The second server continues to be used until it becomes unavailable, and then the FortiGate returns to the first server, if it is available. If both servers are unavailable, then the health check fails.

You can configure the protocol that is used for status checks, including: Ping, HTTP, DNS, TCP echo, UDP echo, two-way active measurement protocol (TWAMP), TCP connect, and FTP. In the GUI, only Ping, HTTP, and DNS are available.

You can view link quality measurements by going to Network > SD-WAN and selecting the Performance SLAs tab. The table shows the default health checks, the health checks that you configured, and information about each health check. The values shown in the Packet Loss, Latency, and Jitter columns are for the health check server that the FortiGate is currently using. The green up arrows indicate that the server is responding, and does not indicate if the health checks are being met.

To configure a link health monitor in the GUI:

1. Go to Network > SD-WAN, select the Performance SLAs tab, and click Create New.

2. Set a Name for the SLA.

3. Set the Protocol that you need to use for status checks: Ping, HTTP, or DNS.

4. Set Server to the IP addresses of up to two servers that all of the SD-WAN members in the performance SLA can reach.

5. Set Participants to All   SD-WAN   Members,   or select Specify to choose specific SD-WAN members.

6. Set Enable probe packets to enable or disable sending probe packets.

7. Configure SLA Target:

   If the health check is used in an SD-WAN rule that uses Manual or Best   Quality strategies,   enabling SLA Target is optional. If the health check is used in an SD-WAN rule that uses Lowest Cost (SLA) or Maximum Bandwidth (SLA) strategies, then SLA Target is enabled.

   When SLA Target is enabled, configure the following:

   - Latency threshold: Calculated based on last 30 probes (default = 5ms).

   - Jitter threshold: Calculated based on last 30 probes (default = 5ms).

   - Packet Loss threshold: Calculated based on last 100 probes (default = 0%).

8. In the Link Status section configure the following:

   - Check interval: The interval in which the FortiGate checks the interface, in milliseconds (500 - 3600000, default = 500).

   - Failures before inactive: The number of failed status checks before the interface shows as inactive (1 - 3600, default =5). This setting helps prevent flapping, where the system continuously transfers traffic back and forth between links

   - Restore link after: The number of successful status checks before the interface shows as active (1 - 3600, default = 5). This setting helps prevent flapping, where the system continuously transfers traffic back and forth between links

9. In the Actions when Inactive section, enable Update static route to disable static routes for inactive interfaces and restore routes when interfaces recover.

10. Click OK.

To configure a link health monitor in the CLI:

config system sdwan

  config health-check

    edit "PingSLA"

      set addr-mode {ipv4 | ipv6}

      set server <server1_IP_address> <server2_IP_address>

      set detect-mode {active | passive | prefer-passive}

      set protocol {ping | tcp-echo | udp-echo | http | twamp | dns | tcp-connect | ftp}

      set ha-priority <integer>

      set probe-timeout <integer>

      set probe-count <integer>

      set probe-packets {enable | disable}

      set interval <integer>

      set failtime <integer>

      set recoverytime <integer>

      set diffservcode <binary>

      set update-static-route {enable | disable}

```
set update-cascade-interface {enable | disable}
set sla-fail-log-period <integer>
set sla-pass-log-period <integer>
set threshold-warning-packetloss <integer>
set threshold-alert-packetloss <integer>
set threshold-warning-latency <integer>
set threshold-alert-latency <integer>
set threshold-warning-jitter <integer>
set threshold-alert-jitter <integer>
set members <member_number> ... <member_number>
config sla
    edit 1
        set link-cost-factor {latency jitter packet-loss}
        set latency-threshold <integer>
        set jitter-threshold <integer>
        set packetloss-threshold <integer>
    next
end
next
end
end
```

Additional settings are available for some of the protocols:

Protocol	Additional options
http	port <port_number>
	http-get <url>
	http-match <response_string>

Protocol	Additional options
twamp	port <port_number> security mode {none | authentication} password <password> packet-size <size>
ftp	ftp {passive | port} ftp-file <path>

Factory default health checks

There are six predefined performance SLA profiles for newly created VDOMs or factory reset FortiGate devices:

- AWS
- System DNS
- FortiGuard
- Gmail
- Google Search
- Office 365

You can view and configure the SLA profiles by going to Network > SD-WAN and selecting the Performance SLAs tab.

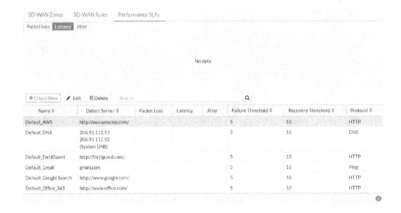

After configuring a health check, you will be able to view packet loss, latency, and jitter data for the SLA profiles. If a value is colored red, it means that it failed to meet the SLA requirements.

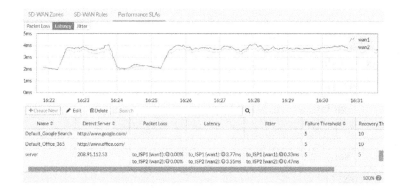

To configure the performance SLA profiles in the CLI:

config system sdwan

  config health-check

    edit "Default_DNS"

      set system-dns enable

      set interval 1000

      set probe-timeout 1000

      set recoverytime 10

      config sla

        edit 1

          set latency-threshold 250

          set jitter-threshold 50

          set packetloss-threshold 5

        next

      end

    next

    edit "Default_Office_365"

      set server "www.office.com"

      set protocol http

      set interval 1000

```
        set probe-timeout 1000
        set recoverytime 10
        config sla
          edit 1
            set latency-threshold 250
            set jitter-threshold 50
            set packetloss-threshold 5
          next
        end
    next
    edit "Default_Gmail"
        set server "gmail.com"
        set interval 1000
        set probe-timeout 1000
        set recoverytime 10
        config sla
          edit 1
            set latency-threshold 250
            set jitter-threshold 50
            set packetloss-threshold 2
          next
        end
    next
    edit "Default_AWS"
        set server "aws.amazon.com"
        set protocol http
        set interval 1000
        set probe-timeout 1000
        set recoverytime 10
        config sla
          edit 1
```

```
              set latency-threshold 250
              set jitter-threshold 50
              set packetloss-threshold 5
          next
      end
  next
  edit "Default_Google Search"
      set server "www.google.com"
      set protocol http
      set interval 1000
      set probe-timeout 1000
      set recoverytime 10
      config sla
          edit 1
              set latency-threshold 250
              set jitter-threshold 50
              set packetloss-threshold 5
          next
      end
  next
  edit "Default_FortiGuard"
      set server "fortiguard.com"
      set protocol http
      set interval 1000
      set probe-timeout 1000
      set recoverytime 10
      config sla
          edit 1
              set latency-threshold 250
              set jitter-threshold 50
              set packetloss-threshold 5
```

```
        next
      end
    next
  end
end
```

Health check options

Health checks include several protocols and protocol specific options. The health check protocol options include:

ping	Use PING to test the link with the server.
tcp-echo	Use TCP echo to test the link with the server.
udp-echo	Use UDP echo to test the link with the server.
http	Use HTTP-GET to test the link with the server.
twamp	Use TWAMP to test the link with the server.
dns	Use DNS query to test the link with the server. The FortiGate sends a DNS query for an A Record and the response matches the expected IP address.
tcp-connect	Use a full TCP connection to test the link with the server. The method to measure the quality of the TCP connection can be: • half-open: FortiGate sends SYN and gets SYN-ACK. The latency is based on the round trip between SYN and SYN-ACK (default). • half-close: FortiGate sends FIN and gets FIN-ACK. The latency is based on the round trip between FIN and FIN-ACK.
ftp	Use FTP to test the link with the server. The FTP mode can be: • passive: The FTP health-check initiates and establishes the data connection (default). • port: The FTP server initiates and establishes the data connection.

SD-WAN health checks can generate traffic that becomes quite high as deployments grow. Please take this into consideration when setting DoS policy thresholds.

To use UDP-echo and TCP-echo as health checks:

```
config system sdwan
    set status enable
    config health-check
        edit "h4_udp1"
            set protocol udp-echo
            set port 7
            set server <server>
        next
        edit "h4_tcp1"
            set protocol tcp-echo
            set port 7
            set server <server>
        next
        edit "h6_udp1"
            set addr-mode ipv6
            set server "2032::12"
            set protocol udp-echo
            set port 7
        next
    end
end
```

To use DNS as a health check, and define the IP address that the response must match:

```
config system sdwan
    set status enable
    config health-check
```

```
    edit "h4_dns1"
       set protocol dns
       set dns-request-domain "ip41.forti2.com"
       set dns-match-ip 1.1.1.1
    next
    edit "h6_dns1"
       set addr-mode ipv6
       set server "2000::15.1.1.4"
       set protocol dns
       set port 53
       set dns-request-domain "ip61.xxx.com"
    next
  end
end
```

To use TCP Open (SYN/SYN-ACK) and TCP Close (FIN/FIN-ACK) to verify connections:

```
config system sdwan
  set status enable
  config health-check
    edit "h4_tcpconnect1"
       set protocol tcp-connect
       set port 443
       set quality-measured-method {half-open | half-close}
       set server <server>
    next
    edit "h6_tcpconnect1"
       set addr-mode ipv6
       set server "2032::13"
       set protocol tcp-connect
```

```
            set port 444
            set quality-measured-method {half-open | half-close}
        next
    end
end


To use active or passive mode FTP to verify connections:


config system sdwan
    set status enable
    config health-check
        edit "h4_ftp1"
            set protocol ftp
            set port 21
            set user "root"
            set password ***********
            set ftp-mode {passive | port}
            set ftp-file "1.txt"
            set server <server>
        next
        edit "h6_ftp1"
            set addr-mode ipv6
            set server "2032::11"
            set protocol ftp
            set port 21
            set user "root"
            set password ***********
            set ftp-mode {passive | port}
            set ftp-file "2.txt"
        next
```

```
        end
end
```

Link monitoring example

Performance SLA link monitoring measures the health of links that are connected to SD-WAN member interfaces by sending probing signals through each link to a server and measuring the link quality based on latency, jitter, and packet loss. If a link is broken, the routes on that link are removed, and traffic is routed through other links. When the link is working again, the routes are reenabbled. This prevents traffic being sent to a broken link and lost.

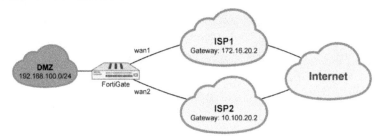

In this example:

- Interfaces wan1 and wan2 connect to the internet through separate ISPs
- The detection server IP address is 208.91.114.182

A performance SLA is created so that, if one link fails, its routes are removed and traffic is detoured to the other link.

To configure a Performance SLA using the GUI:

2. On the FortiGate, add wan1 and wan2 as SD-WAN members, then add a policy and static route. Go to Network > SD-WAN, select the Performance SLAs tab, and click Create New.

3. Enter a name for the SLA and select a protocol.

4. In the Server field, enter the detection server IP address (208.91.114.182 in this example).

5. In the Participants field, select both wan1 and wan2.

6. Configured the remaining settings as needed, then click OK.

To configure a Performance SLA using the CLI:

config system sdwan

```
config health-check
    edit "server"
        set server "208.91.114.182"
        set update-static-route enable
        set members 1 2
    next
end
end
```

To diagnose the Performance SLA status:

 # diagnose sys sdwan health-check

Health Check(server):

Seq(1): state(alive), packet-loss(0.000%) latency(15.247), jitter(5.231) sla_map=0x0

Seq(2): state(alive), packet-loss(0.000%) latency(13.621), jitter(6.905) sla_map=0x0

SLA targets example

SLA targets are a set of constraints that are used in SD-WAN rules to control the paths that traffic take.

The available constraints are:

- Latency threshold: Latency for SLA to make decision, in milliseconds (0 - 10000000, default = 5).

- Jitter threshold: Jitter for SLA to make decision, in milliseconds (0 - 10000000, default = 5).

- Packet loss threshold: Packet loss for SLA to make decision, in percentage (0 - 100, default = 0).

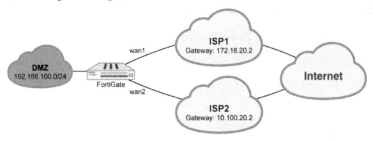

To configure Performance SLA targets using the GUI:

1. On the FortiGate, add wan1 and wan2 as SD-WAN members, then add a policy and static route.

2. Go to Network > SD-WAN and select the Performance SLAs tab.

4. Create a new Performance SLA or edit an existing one. Enable SLA Targetsand configure the constraints. To add multiple SLA targets, use the CLI.

5. Configured the remaining settings as needed, then click OK.

To configure Performance SLA targets using the CLI:

config system sdwan
   config health-check
     edit "server"
       set server "208.91.114.182"

```
set members 1 2
config sla
    edit 1
        set link-cost-factor latency jitter packet-loss
        set latency-threshold 10
        set jitter-threshold 10
        set packetloss-threshold 1
    next
    edit 2
        set link-cost-factor latency packet-loss
        set latency-threshold 15
        set packetloss-threshold 2
    next
    end
  next
 end
end
```

The link-cost-factor variable is used to select which constraints are enabled.

Passive WAN health measurement

SD-WAN passive WAN health measurement determines the health check measurements using session information that is captured on firewall policies that have Passive Health Check (passive-wan-health-measurement) enabled. Passive measurements analyze session information that is gathered from various TCP sessions to determine the jitter, latency, and packet loss.

Using passive WAN health measurement reduces the amount of configuration required and decreases the traffic that is produced by health check monitor probes doing active measurements. Passive WAN health measurement analyzes real-life traffic; active WAN health measurement using a detection server might not reflect the real-life traffic.

By default, active WAN health measurement is enabled when a new health check is created. It can be changed to passive or prefer passive:

passive	Health is measured using traffic, without probes. No link health monitor needs to be configured.
prefer-passive	Health is measured using traffic when there is traffic, and using probes when there is no traffic. A link health monitor must be configured.

When passive-wan-health-measurement is enabled, auto-asic-offload will be disabled.

Example

In this example, the FortiGate is configured to load-balance between two WAN interfaces, port15 and port16. A health check is configured in passive mode, and SLA thresholds are set. Passive WAN health measurement is enabled on the SD-WAN policy.

Measurements are taken from YouTube traffic generated by the PC. When latency is introduced to the traffic on port15, the passive health check trigger threshold is exceeded and traffic is rerouted to port16.

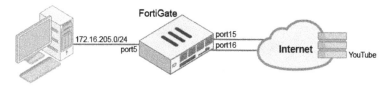

To configure the SD-WAN in the GUI:

1. Create the SD-WAN zone:

   1. Go to Network > SD-WAN and select the SD-WAN Zones tab.

   2. Click Create New > SD-WAN Zone.

   3. Enter a name for the zone, such as SD-WAN.

   4. Click OK.

2. Create the SD-WAN members:

   1. Go to Network > SD-WAN and select the SD-WAN Zones tab.

   2. Click Create New > SD-WAN Member.

   3. Set Interface to port15, SD-WAN Zone to SD-WAN, and Gateway set to 172.16.209.2.

   4. Click OK.

   5. Click Create New > SD-WAN Member again.

   6. Set Interface to port16, SD-WAN Zone to SD-WAN, and Gateway set to 172.16.210.2.

   7. Click OK.

3. Create a performance SLA:

   1. Go to Network > SD-WAN and select the Performance SLAs tab.

   2. Edit an existing health check, or create a new one.

   3. Set Probe mode to Passive.

   4. Set Participants to Specify and add port15 and port16.

   5. Configure two SLA targets. Note that the second SLA target must be configured in the CLI.

59

6. Configure the remaining settings as needed.

7. Click OK.

   The SLA list shows the probe mode in the Detect Server column, if the probe mode is passive or prefer passive.

Probe packets can only be disabled in the CLI and when the probe mode is not passive.

4. Create SD-WAN rules:

   1. Go to Network > SD-WAN, select the SD-WAN Rules tab, and click Create New.

   2. Configure the first rule:

Name	Background_Traffic
Source address	172.16.205.0
Application	Click in the field, and in the Select Entries pane search for YouTube and select all of the entries
Strategy	Maximize Bandwidth (SLA)
Interface	port15 and port16

preference

Required SLA target	Passive_Check#2

3. Click OK.

4. Click Create New again and configure the second rule:

Name	Foreground_Traffic
Source address	172.16.205.0
Address	all
Protocol number	Specify - 1
Strategy	Lowest Cost (SLA)
Interface preference	port15 and port16
Required SLA target	Passive_Check#1

5. Click OK.

To configure the firewall policy in the GUI:

1. Go to Policy & Objects > Firewall Policy and click Create New.

2. Configure the policy:

Name	SD-WAN-HC-policy
Incoming Interface	port5
Outgoing Interface	SD-WAN
Source	all

Destination	all
Schedule	always
Service	ALL
Action	ACCEPT
Passive Health Check	Enabled Passive health check can only be enabled in a policy when the outgoing interface is an SD-WAN zone.

    3.   Click OK.

To configure the SD-WAN in the CLI:

```
config system sdwan
  set status enable
  config zone
    edit "SD-WAN"
    next
  end
  config members
    edit 1
      set zone "SD-WAN"
      set interface "port15"
      set gateway 172.16.209.2
    next
    edit 2
      set zone "SD-WAN"
      set interface "port16"
      set gateway 172.16.210.2
```

```
        next
    end
    config health-check
        edit "Passive_Check"
            set detect-mode passive
            set members 1 2
            config sla
                edit 1
                    set latency-threshold 500
                    set jitter-threshold 500
                    set packetloss-threshold 10
                next
                edit 2
                    set latency-threshold 1000
                    set jitter-threshold 1000
                    set packetloss-threshold 10
                next
            end
        next
    end
    config service
        edit 1
            set name "Background_Traffic"
            set mode load-balance
            set src "172.16.205.0"
            set internet-service enable
            set internet-service-app-ctrl 31077 33321 41598 31076 33104
23397 30201 16420 17396 38569 25564
            config sla
                edit "Passive_Check"
                    set id 2
```

63

```
            next
        end
        set priority-member 1 2
    next
    edit 2
        set name "Foreground_Traffic"
        set mode sla
        set src "172.16.205.0"
        set protocol 1
        set dst "all"
        config sla
            edit "Passive_Check"
                set id 1
            next
        end
        set priority-member 1 2
    next
  end
end
```

To configure the firewall policy in the CLI:

```
config firewall policy
    edit 1
        set name "SD-WAN-HC-policy"
        set srcintf "port5"
        set dstintf "SD-WAN"
        set nat enable
        set srcaddr "all"
        set dstaddr "all"
        set action accept
```

set schedule "always"

set service "ALL"

set passive-wan-health-measurement enable

set auto-asic-offload disable

next

end

Results

When both links pass the SLA:

diagnose sys link-monitor-passive interface

Interface port16 (28):

  Latency 10.000 Jitter 5.000 Packet_loss 0.000% Last_updated Fri Mar 5 10:09:21 2021

Interface port15 (27):

  Latency 60.000 Jitter 0.000 Packet_loss 0.000% Last_updated Fri Mar 5 10:39:24 2021

diagnose sys sdwan health-check

Health Check(Passive_Check):

Seq(1 port15): state(alive), packet-loss(0.000%) latency(60.000), jitter(0.750) sla_map=0x3

Seq(2 port16): state(alive), packet-loss(0.000%) latency(10.000), jitter(5.000) sla_map=0x3

diagnose sys sdwan service 2

Service(2): Address Mode(IPV4) flags=0x200

  Gen(1), TOS(0x0/0x0), Protocol(1: 1->65535), Mode(sla), sla-compare-order

  Members(2):

   1: Seq_num(1 port15), alive, sla(0x1), gid(0), cfg_order(0), cost(0), selected

   2: Seq_num(2 port16), alive, sla(0x1), gid(0), cfg_order(1), cost(0), selected

Src address(1):

   172.16.205.0-172.16.205.255

Dst address(1):

   8.8.8.8-8.8.8.8

When the latency is increased to 610ms on port15, the SLA is broken and pings are sent on port16:

diagnose sys sdwan health-check

Health Check(Passive_Check):

Seq(1 port15): state(alive), packet-loss(0.000%) latency(610.000), jitter(2.500) sla_map=0x3

Seq(2 port16): state(alive), packet-loss(0.000%) latency(50.000), jitter(21.000) sla_map=0x3

diagnose sys sdwan service 2

Service(2): Address Mode(IPV4) flags=0x200

   Gen(6), TOS(0x0/0x0), Protocol(1: 1->65535), Mode(sla), sla-compare-order

   Members(2):

   1: Seq_num(2 port16), alive, sla(0x1), gid(1), cfg_order(1), cost(0), selected

   2: Seq_num(1 port15), alive, sla(0x0), gid(2), cfg_order(0), cost(0), selected

   Src address(1):

      172.16.205.0-172.16.205.255

   Dst address(1):

      8.8.8.8-8.8.8.8

Passive health-check measurement by internet service and application

Passive health measurement supports passive detection for each internet service and application.

If internet services or applications are defined in an SD-WAN rule with passive health check, SLA information for each service or application will be differentiated and collected. SLA metrics (latency, jitter, and packet loss) on each SD-WAN member in the rule are then calculated based on the relevant internet service's or application's SLA information.

In this example, three SD-WAN rules are created:

- Rule 1: Best quality (latency) using passive SLA for the internet services Alibaba and Amazon.

- Rule 2: Best quality (latency) using passive SLA for the applications Netflix and YouTube.

- Rule 3: Best quality (latency) using passive SLA for all other traffic.

After passive application measurement is enabled for rules one and two, the SLA metric of rule one is the average latency of the internet services Alibaba and Amazon, and the SLA metric of rule two is the average latency of the applications Netflix and YouTube.

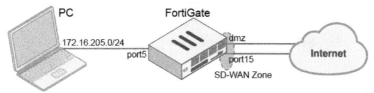

To configure the SD-WAN:

Configure the SD-WAN members:

config system sdwan

  set status enable

  config zone

    edit "virtual-wan-link"

    next

  end

  config members

```
    edit 1
        set interface "dmz"
        set gateway 172.16.208.2
    next
    edit 2
        set interface "port15"
        set gateway 172.16.209.2
    next
  end
            end
```

Configure the passive mode health check:

```
config health-check
    edit "Passive_HC"
      set detect-mode passive
      set members 1 2
    next
            end
```

Configure SD-WAN service rules:

```
config service
    edit 1
        set name "1"
        set mode priority
        set src "172.16.205.0"
        set internet-service enable
        set internet-service-name "Alibaba-Web" "Amazon-Web"
        set health-check "Passive_HC"
        set priority-members 1 2
```

```
    set passive-measurement enable    //Enable "passive application
measurement", it is a new command which is introduced in this
project.

    next

    edit 2

        set name "2"

        set mode priority

        set src "172.16.205.0"

        set internet-service enable

        set internet-service-app-ctrl 18155 31077

        set health-check "Passive_HC"

        set priority-members 1 2

        set passive-measurement enable        ////Enable "passive
application measurement"

    next

    edit 3

        set name "3"

        set mode priority

        set dst "all"

        set src "172.16.205.0"

        set health-check "Passive_HC"

        set priority-members 1 2

    next

                    end
```

Configure SD-WAN routes:

```
config router static

    edit 1

        set distance 1

        set sdwan-zone "virtual-wan-link"

    next

                    end
```

Configure the firewall policy with passive WAN health measurement enabled:

config firewall policy
    edit 1
        set uuid 972345c6-1595-51ec-66c5-d705d266f712
        set srcintf "port5"
        set dstintf "virtual-wan-link"
        set action accept
        set srcaddr "172.16.205.0"
        set dstaddr "all"
        set schedule "always"
        set service "ALL"
        set passive-wan-health-measurement enable
        set utm-status enable
        set ssl-ssh-profile "certificate-inspection"
        set application-list "g-default"
        set auto-asic-offload disable
    next
        end

To verify the results:

1. On the PC, open the browser and visit the internet services and applications.

2. On the FortiGate, check the collected SLA information to confirm that each server or application on the SD-WAN members was measured individually:

diagnose sys link-monitor-passive interface

Interface dmz (5):

    Default(0x00000000): latency=3080.0 11:57:54, jitter=5.0 11:58:08, pktloss=0.0 % NA

Alibaba-Web(0x00690001): latency=30.0   11:30:06, jitter=25.0 11:29:13, pktloss=0.0 % NA

YouTube(0x00007965): latency=100.0   12:00:35, jitter=2.5 12:00:30, pktloss=0.0 % NA

Netflix(0x000046eb): latency=10.0   11:31:24, jitter=10.0 11:30:30, pktloss=0.0 % NA

Amazon-Web(0x00060001): latency=80.0   11:31:52, jitter=35.0 11:32:07, pktloss=0.0 % NA

Interface port15 (27):

Default(0x00000000): latency=100.0   12:00:42, jitter=0.0 12:00:42, pktloss=0.0 % NA

Amazon-Web(0x00060001): latency=30.0   11:56:05, jitter=0.0 11:55:21, pktloss=0.0 % NA

Alibaba-Web(0x00690001): latency=0.0   11:26:08, jitter=35.0 11:27:08, pktloss=0.0 % NA

YouTube(0x00007965): latency=100.0   11:33:34, jitter=0.0 11:33:50, pktloss=0.0 % NA

Netflix(0x000046eb): latency=0.0   11:26:29, jitter=0.0   11:29:03, pktloss=0.0 % NA

Verify that the SLA metrics on the members are calculated as expected:

diagnose sys sdwan service

Service(1): Address Mode(IPV4) flags=0x600 use-shortcut-sla

Gen(1), TOS(0x0/0x0), Protocol(0: 1->65535), Mode(priority), link-cost-factor(latency), link-cost-threshold(10), heath-check(Passive_HC)

Members(2):

1: Seq_num(2 port15), alive, latency: 15.000, selected   // Average latency of "Alibaba-Web" and "Amazon-Web" on port15: 15.000 = (0.0+30.0)/2

2: Seq_num(1 dmz), alive, latency: 55.000, selected   // Average latency of "Alibaba-Web" and "Amazon-Web" on dmz: 55.000 = (30.0+80.0)/2

Internet Service(2): Alibaba-Web(6881281,0,0,0) Amazon-Web(393217,0,0,0)

Src address(1):

172.16.205.0-172.16.205.255

Service(2): Address Mode(IPV4) flags=0x600 use-shortcut-sla

Gen(2), TOS(0x0/0x0), Protocol(0: 1->65535), Mode(priority), link-cost-factor(latency), link-cost-threshold(10), heath-check(Passive_HC)

Members(2):

1: Seq_num(1 dmz), alive, latency: 55.000, selected   // Average latency of "Netflix" and "YouTube" on dmz: 55.000 = (10.0+100.0)/2

2: Seq_num(2 port15), alive, latency: 50.000, selected   // Average latency of "Netflix" and "YouTube" on port15:   50.000 = (0.0+100.0)/2

Internet Service(2): Netflix(4294837427,0,0,0 18155) YouTube(4294838283,0,0,0 31077)

Src address(1):

172.16.205.0-172.16.205.255

Service(3): Address Mode(IPV4) flags=0x200 use-shortcut-sla

Gen(9), TOS(0x0/0x0), Protocol(0: 1->65535), Mode(priority), link-cost-factor(latency), link-cost-threshold(10), heath-check(Passive_HC)

Members(2):

1: Seq_num(2 port15), alive, latency: 46.000, selected   // Average latency of all TCP traffic on port15:   46 = (100.0+30.0+0.0+100.0+0.0)/5

2: Seq_num(1 dmz), alive, latency: 660.000, selected   // Average latency of all TCP traffic on dmz: 660 = (3080.0+30.0+100.0+10.0+80.0)/5

Src address(1):

172.16.205.0-172.16.205.255

Dst address(1):

     0.0.0.0-255.255.255.255

Health check packet DSCP marker support

SD-WAN health check probe packets support Differentiated Services Code Point (DSCP) markers for accurate evaluation of the link performance for high priority applications by upstream devices.

When the SD-WAN health check packet is sent out, the DSCP can be set with a CLI command.

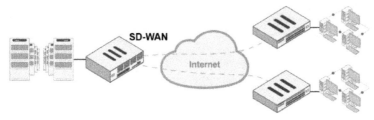

To mark health-check packets with DSCP:

config system sdwan
    config health-check
        edit <name>
            set diffservcode <6 bits binary, range 000000-111111>
        next
    end
end

Manual interface speedtest

An interface speedtest can be manually performed on WAN interfaces in the GUI. The results of the test can be added to the interface's Estimated bandwidth. The estimated upstream and downstream bandwidths can be used in SD-WAN service rules to determine the best link to use when either Maximize Bandwidth or Best Quality strategies are selected.

An SD-WAN Network Monitor license is required to use the speedtest. The License widget and the System > FortiGuard page show the license status.

To run an interface speedtest in the GUI:

1. Go to Network > Interfaces.

2. Edit a WAN interface. The interfaces can be grouped by role using the grouping dropdown on the right side of the toolbar.

3. Click Execute speed test in the right pane.

4. When the test completes, click OK in the Confirm pane to apply the results to the estimated bandwidth.

   The results can also be applied later by clicking Apply results to estimated bandwidth.

   The speedtest results are used to populate the Estimated bandwidth fields.

5. Click OK.

The FortiGate must be connected to FortiGuard, and able to reach either the AWS or Google speedtest servers.

Scheduled interface speedtest

The SD-WAN Network Monitor service supports running a speed test based on a schedule. The test results are automatically updated in the interface measured-upstream-bandwidth and measured-downstream-bandwidth fields. These fields do not impact the interface inbound bandwidth, outbound bandwidth, estimated upstream bandwidth, or estimated downstream bandwidth settings.

An SD-WAN Network Monitor license is required to use the speedtest. The License widget and the System > FortiGuard page show the license status.

When the scheduled speed tests run, it is possible to temporarily bypass the bandwidth limits set on the interface and configure custom maximum or minimum bandwidth limits. These configurations are optional.

config system speed-test-schedule

    edit <interface>

        set schedules <schedule> ...

        set update-inbandwidth enable {enable | disable}

        set update-outbandwidth enable {enable | disable}

        set update-inbandwidth-maximum <integer>

        set update-inbandwidth-minimum <integer>

        set update-outbandwidth-maximum <integer>

        set update-outbandwidth-minimum <integer>

    next

end

update-inbandwidth enable {enable | disable}	Enable/disable bypassing the interface's inbound bandwidth setting.
update-outbandwidth enable {enable | disable}	Enable/disable bypassing the interface's outbound bandwidth setting.
update-inbandwidth-maximum <integer>	Maximum downloading bandwidth to be used in a speed test, in Kbps (0 - 16776000).

update-inbandwidth- minimum \<integer\>	Minimum downloading bandwidth to be considered effective, in Kbps (0 - 16776000).
update-outbandwidth- maximum \<integer\>	Maximum uploading bandwidth to be used in a speed test, in Kbps (0 - 16776000).
update-outbandwidth- minimum \<integer\>	Minimum uploading bandwidth to be considered effective, in Kbps (0 - 16776000).

In the following example, a speed test is scheduled on port1 at 10:00 AM, and another one at 14:00 PM.

To run a speed test based on a schedule:

Configure the recurring schedules:

```
config firewall schedule recurring
    edit "10"
        set start 10:00
        set end 12:00
        set day monday tuesday wednesday thursday friday
    next
    edit "14"
        set start 14:00
        set end 16:00
        set day monday tuesday wednesday thursday friday
    next
                end
```

Configure the speed test schedule:

```
config system speed-test-schedule
    edit "port1"
```

```
        set schedules "10" "14"
        set update-inbandwidth enable
        set update-outbandwidth enable
        set update-inbandwidth-maximum 60000
        set update-inbandwidth-minimum 10000
        set update-outbandwidth-maximum 50000
        set update-outbandwidth-minimum 10000
    next
            end
```

View the speed test results:

```
config system interface
    edit port1
        get | grep measure
            measured-upstream-bandwidth: 23691
            measured-downstream-bandwidth: 48862
            bandwidth-measure-time:  Wed Jan 27 14:00:39 2021
    next
            end
```

Monitor performance SLA

SD-WAN diagnostics can be used to help maintain your SD-WAN solution

Monitoring SD-WAN link quality status

Link quality plays a significant role in link selection for SD-WAN. Investigate any prolonged issues with packet loss, latency, or jitter to ensure that your network does not experience degraded performance or an outage.

You can monitor the link quality status of SD-WAN interface members by going to Network > SD-WAN and selecting the Performance SLAs tab.

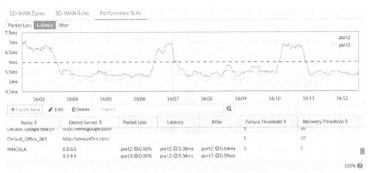

The live charts show the packet loss, latency, or jitter for the selected health check. Hover the cursor over a line in the chart to see the specific value for that interface at that specific time.

The table shows information about each health check, including the configured servers, link quality data, and thresholds. The colored arrow indicates the status of the interface when the last status check was performed: green means that the interface was active, and red means that the interface was inactive. Hover the cursor over the arrow for additional information.

Monitoring system event logs

The features adds an SD-WAN daemon function to keep a short, 10 minute history of SLA that can be viewed in the CLI.

Performance SLA results related to interface selection, session failover, and other information, can be logged. These logs can then be used for long-term monitoring of traffic issues at remote sites, and for reports and views in FortiAnalyzer.

The time intervals that Performance SLA fail and pass logs are generated in can be configured.

To configure the fail and pass logs' generation time interval:

```
config system sdwan
    config health-check
        edit "PingSLA"
            set sla-fail-log-period 30
            set sla-pass-log-period 60
        next
    end
end
```

To view the 10 minute Performance SLA link status history:

FGDocs # diagnose sys sdwan sla-log PingSLA 1

Timestamp: Fri Sep 4 10:32:37 2020, vdom root, health-check PingSLA, interface: wan2, status: up, latency: 4.455, jitter: 0.430, packet loss: 0.000%.

Timestamp: Fri Sep 4 10:32:37 2020, vdom root, health-check PingSLA, interface: wan2, status: up, latency: 4.461, jitter: 0.436, packet loss: 0.000%.

Timestamp: Fri Sep 4 10:32:38 2020, vdom root, health-check PingSLA, interface: wan2, status: up, latency: 4.488, jitter: 0.415, packet loss: 0.000%.

...

Timestamp: Fri Sep 4 10:42:36 2020, vdom root, health-check PingSLA, interface: wan2, status: up, latency: 6.280, jitter: 0.302, packet loss: 0.000%.

Timestamp: Fri Sep 4 10:42:37 2020, vdom root, health-check PingSLA, interface: wan2, status: up, latency: 6.261, jitter: 0.257, packet loss: 0.000%.

Timestamp: Fri Sep 4 10:42:37 2020, vdom root, health-check PingSLA, interface: wan2, status: up, latency: 6.229, jitter: 0.245, packet loss: 0.000%.

SLA pass logs

The FortiGate generates Performance SLA logs at the specified pass log interval (sla-pass-log-period) when SLA passes.

date="2021-04-15" time="10:04:56" id=6951431609690095758 bid=52507 dvid=1047 itime=1618506296 euid=3 epid=3 dsteuid=3 dstepid=3 logver=700000066 logid="0113022925" type="event" subtype="sdwan" level="information" msg="Health Check SLA status." logdesc="SDWAN SLA information" status="up" interface="port1" eventtime=1618506296222639301 tz="-0700" eventtype="SLA" jitter="0.277" inbandwidthavailable="10.00Gbps" outbandwidthavailable="10.00Gbps" bibandwidthavailable="20.00Gbps" packetloss="1.000%" latency="186.071" slamap="0x1" healthcheck="BusinessCritical_CloudApps" slatargetid=1 outbandwidthused="40kbps" inbandwidthused="24kbps" bibandwidthused="64kbps" devid="FGVM02TM20000000" vd="root" devname="Branch_Office_01" csf="fabric"

date="2021-04-15" time="10:04:56" id=6951431609690095759 bid=52507 dvid=1047 itime=1618506296 euid=3 epid=3 dsteuid=3 dstepid=3 logver=700000066 logid="0113022925" type="event" subtype="sdwan" level="information" msg="Health Check SLA status." logdesc="SDWAN SLA information" status="up" interface="port2" eventtime=1618506296223163068 tz="-0700" eventtype="SLA" jitter="0.204" inbandwidthavailable="10.00Gbps" outbandwidthavailable="10.00Gbps" bibandwidthavailable="20.00Gbps" packetloss="0.000%" latency="185.939" slamap="0x1" healthcheck="BusinessCritical_CloudApps" slatargetid=1 outbandwidthused="142kbps" inbandwidthused="23kbps" bibandwidthused="165kbps" devid="FGVM02TM20000000" vd="root" devname="Branch_Office_01" csf="fabric"

In the FortiAnalyzer GUI:

82

SLA fail logs

The FortiGate generates Performance SLA logs at the specified fail log interval (sla-fail-log-period) when SLA fails.

date="2021-04-15" time="10:04:59" id=6951431618280030243 bid=52507 dvid=1047 itime=1618506298 euid=3 epid=3 dsteuid=3 dstepid=3 logver=700000066 logid="0113022925" type="event" subtype="sdwan" level="notice" msg="Health Check SLA status. SLA failed due to being over the performance metric threshold." logdesc="SDWAN SLA information" status="down" interface="To-HQ-MPLS" eventtime=1618506299718862835 tz="-0700" eventtype="SLA" jitter="0.000" inbandwidthavailable="10.00Gbps" outbandwidthavailable="10.00Gbps" bibandwidthavailable="20.00Gbps" packetloss="100.000%" latency="0.000" slamap="0x0" healthcheck="BusinessCritical_CloudApps" slatargetid=1 metric="packetloss" outbandwidthused="0kbps" inbandwidthused="0kbps" bibandwidthused="0kbps" devid="FGVM02TM20000000" vd="root" devname="Branch_Office_01" csf="fabric"

date="2021-04-15" time="10:05:03" id=6951431639754866704 bid=52514 dvid=1046 itime=1618506303 euid=3 epid=3 dsteuid=3 dstepid=3 logver=700000066 logid="0113022925" type="event" subtype="sdwan" level="notice" msg="Health Check SLA status. SLA failed due to being over the performance metric threshold." logdesc="SDWAN SLA information" status="down" interface="To-HQ-MPLS" eventtime=1618506304085863643 tz="-0700" eventtype="SLA" jitter="0.000" inbandwidthavailable="10.00Gbps" outbandwidthavailable="10.00Gbps" bibandwidthavailable="20.00Gbps" packetloss="100.000%" latency="0.000" slamap="0x0" healthcheck="BusinessCritical_CloudApps" slatargetid=1 metric="packetloss" outbandwidthused="6kbps" inbandwidthused="3kbps" bibandwidthused="9kbps" devid="FGVM02TM20000000" vd="root" devname="Branch_Office_02" csf="fabric"

In the FortiAnalyzer GUI:

SLA monitoring using the REST API

SLA log information and interface SLA information can be monitored using the REST API. This feature is also be used by FortiManager as part of its detailed SLA monitoring and drill-down features.

Interface log command example:

https://172.172.172.9/api/v2/monitor/virtual-wan/interface-log

```
{
  "http_method":"GET",
  "results":[
   {
     "interface":"port13",
     "logs":[
      {
        "timestamp":1547087168,
        "tx_bandwidth":3447,
        "rx_bandwidth":3457,
        "bi_bandwidth":6904,
        "tx_bytes":748875,
        "rx_bytes":708799,
        "egress_queue":[
        ]
      },
      {
        "timestamp":1547087178,
        "tx_bandwidth":3364,
        "rx_bandwidth":3400,
        "bi_bandwidth":6764,
        "tx_bytes":753789,
        "rx_bytes":712835,
        "egress_queue":[
        ]
```

```
        },
....

....
```

SLA log command example:

https://172.172.172.9/api/v2/monitor/virtual-wan/sla-log

```
{
  "http_method":"GET",
  "results":[
    {
      "name":"ping",
      "interface":"spoke11-p1",
      "logs":[
        {
          "timestamp":1614813142,
          "link":"up",
          "latency":0.13763333857059479,
          "jitter":0.02996666356921196,
          "packetloss":0
        },

      "child_intfs":{
        "spoke11-p1_0":[
          {
            "timestamp":1614813142,
            "link":"up",
            "latency":0.12413334846496582,
            "jitter":0.028366668149828911,
            "packetloss":0
          },
```

```json
{
  "name":"ping",
  "interface":"spoke12-p1",
  "logs":[
    {
      "timestamp":1614813143,
      "link":"up",
      "latency":0.11373332887887955,
      "jitter":0.023099998012185097,
      "packetloss":0
    },

  "child_intfs":{
    "spoke12-p1_0":[
      {
        "timestamp":1614813143,
        "link":"up",
        "latency":0.0930333212018013,
        "jitter":0.011033335700631142,
        "packetloss":0
      },
....
....
```

Health check command example:

https://172.172.172.9/api/v2/monitor/virtual-wan/health-check

```json
{
  "http_method":"GET",
  "results":{
    "ping":{
      "spoke11-p1":{
```

"status":"up",
"latency":0.13406667113304138,
"jitter":0.023000005632638931,
"packet_loss":0,
"packet_sent":29722,
"packet_received":29718,
"sla_targets_met":[
  1
],
"session":2,
"tx_bandwidth":1353,
"rx_bandwidth":1536,
"state_changed":1614798274,
"child_intfs":{
  "spoke11-p1_0":{
    "status":"up",
    "latency":0.12929999828338623,
    "jitter":0.028200000524520874,
    "packet_loss":0,
    "packet_sent":29626,
    "packet_received":29625,
    "sla_targets_met":[
      1
    ],
    "session":0,
    "tx_bandwidth":2608,
    "rx_bandwidth":1491,
    "state_changed":0
  }
}
},

"spoke12-p1":{
 "status":"up",
 "latency":0.11356667429208755,
 "jitter":0.015699999406933784,
 "packet_loss":0,
 "packet_sent":29722,
 "packet_received":29717,
 "sla_targets_met":[
  1
 ],
 "session":2,
 "tx_bandwidth":1353,
 "rx_bandwidth":1536,
 "state_changed":1614798274,
 "child_intfs":{
  "spoke12-p1_0":{
   "status":"up",
   "latency":0.095466658473014832,
   "jitter":0.0092999991029500961,
   "packet_loss":0,
   "packet_sent":29687,
   "packet_received":29686,
   "sla_targets_met":[
    1
   ],
   "session":0,
   "tx_bandwidth":1309,
   "rx_bandwidth":2553,
   "state_changed":0
  }
 }
}

```
        }
    }
},
....

....
```

CLI diagnose commands:

diagnose sys sdwan intf-sla-log port13

Timestamp: Wed Jan 9 18:33:49 2019, used inbandwidth: 3208bps, used outbandwidth: 3453bps, used bibandwidth: 6661bps, tx bytes: 947234bytes, rx bytes: 898622bytes.

Timestamp: Wed Jan 9 18:33:59 2019, used inbandwidth: 3317bps, used outbandwidth: 3450bps, used bibandwidth: 6767bps, tx bytes: 951284bytes, rx bytes: 902937bytes.

Timestamp: Wed Jan 9 18:34:09 2019, used inbandwidth: 3302bps, used outbandwidth: 3389bps, used bibandwidth: 6691bps, tx bytes: 956268bytes, rx bytes: 907114bytes.

Timestamp: Wed Jan 9 18:34:19 2019, used inbandwidth: 3279bps, used outbandwidth: 3352bps, used bibandwidth: 6631bps, tx bytes: 958920bytes, rx bytes: 910793bytes.

Timestamp: Wed Jan 9 18:34:29 2019, used inbandwidth: 3233bps, used outbandwidth: 3371bps, used bibandwidth: 6604bps, tx bytes: 964374bytes, rx bytes: 914854bytes.

Timestamp: Wed Jan 9 18:34:39 2019, used inbandwidth: 3235bps, used outbandwidth: 3362bps, used bibandwidth: 6597bps, tx bytes: 968250bytes, rx bytes: 918846bytes.

Timestamp: Wed Jan 9 18:34:49 2019, used inbandwidth: 3165bps, used outbandwidth: 3362bps, used bibandwidth: 6527bps, tx bytes: 972298bytes, rx bytes: 922724bytes.

Timestamp: Wed Jan 9 18:34:59 2019, used inbandwidth: 3184bps, used outbandwidth: 3362bps, used bibandwidth: 6546bps, tx bytes: 977282bytes, rx bytes: 927019bytes.

diagnose sys sdwan sla-log ping 1 spoke11-p1_0

Timestamp: Wed Mar 3 15:35:20 2021, vdom root, health-check ping, interface: spoke11-p1_0, status: up, latency: 0.135, jitter: 0.029, packet loss: 0.000%.

diagnose sys sdwan sla-log ping 2 spoke12-p1_0

Timestamp: Wed Mar 3 15:36:08 2021, vdom root, health-check ping, interface: spoke12-p1_0, status: up, latency: 0.095, jitter: 0.010, packet loss: 0.000%.

diagnose sys sdwan health-check

Health Check(ping):

Seq(1 spoke11-p1): state(alive), packet-loss(0.000%) latency(0.156), jitter(0.043) sla_map=0x1

Seq(1 spoke11-p1_0): state(alive), packet-loss(0.000%) latency(0.128), jitter(0.024) sla_map=0x1

Seq(2 spoke12-p1): state(alive), packet-loss(0.000%) latency(0.125), jitter(0.028) sla_map=0x1

Seq(2 spoke12-p1_0): state(alive), packet-loss(0.000%) latency(0.093), jitter(0.008) sla_map=0x1

Mean opinion score calculation and logging in performance SLA health checks

The mean opinion score (MOS) is a method of measuring voice quality using a formula that takes latency, jitter, packet loss, and the codec into account to produce a score from zero to five (0 - 5). The G.711, G.729, and G.722 codecs can be selected in the health check configurations, and an MOS threshold can be entered to indicate the minimum MOS score for the SLA to pass. The maximum MOS score will depend on which codec is used, since each codec has a theoretical maximum limit.

```
config system sdwan
    config health-check
        edit <name>
        set mos-codec {g711 | g729 | g722}
        config sla
            edit <id>
                set link-cost-factor {latency jitter packet-loss mos}
                set mos-threshold <value>
            next
        end
    next
    end
end
```

mos-codec {g711 | g729 | g722}	Set the VoIP codec to use for the MOS calculation (default = g711).
link-cost-factor {latency jitter packet-loss mos}	Set the criteria to base the link selection on.
mos-threshold <value>	Set the minimum MOS for the SLA to be marked as pass (1.0 - 5.0, default = 3.6).

To configure a health check to calculate the MOS:

```
config system sdwan
    set status enable
    config zone
        edit "virtual-wan-link"
        next
    end
    config members
        edit 1
            set interface "dmz"
            set gateway 172.16.208.2
        next
        edit 2
            set interface "port15"
            set gateway 172.16.209.2
        next
    end
    config health-check
        edit "Test_MOS"
            set server "2.2.2.2"
            set sla-fail-log-period 30
            set sla-pass-log-period 30
            set members 0
            set mos-codec g729
            config sla
                edit 1
                    set link-cost-factor mos
                    set mos-threshold "4.0"
                next
            end
        next
    end
```

end

To use an MOS SLA to steer traffic in an SD-WAN rule:

config system sdwan
  config service
    edit 1
      set name "MOS_traffic_steering"
      set mode sla
      set dst "HQ_LAN"
      set src "Branch_LAN"
      config sla
        edit "Test_MOS"
          set id 1
        next
      end
      set priority-members 0
    next
  end
end

The MOS currently cannot be used to steer traffic when the mode is set to priority.

To verify the MOS calculation results:

Verify the health check diagnostics:

diagnose sys sdwan health-check

Health Check(Test_MOS):

Seq(1 **dmz**): state(alive), packet-loss(0.000%) latency(0.114), jitter(0.026), **mos(4.123)**, bandwidth-up(999999), bandwidth-dw(999997), bandwidth-bi(1999996) sla_map=0x1

Seq(2 **port15**): state(alive), packet-loss(0.000%) latency(0.100), jitter(0.008), **mos(4.123)**, bandwidth-up(999999), bandwidth-dw(999999), bandwidth-bi(1999998) sla_map=0x1

diagnose sys sdwan sla-log Test_MOS 1

Timestamp: Tue Jan 4 11:23:06 2022, vdom root, health-check Test_MOS, interface: **dmz**, status: up, latency: 0.151, jitter: 0.040, packet loss: 0.000%, **mos: 4.123**.

> Timestamp: Tue Jan 4 11:23:07 2022, vdom root, health-check Test_MOS, interface: **dmz**, status: up, latency: 0.149, jitter: 0.041, packet loss: 0.000%, **mos: 4.123**.
>
> # diagnose sys sdwan sla-log Test_MOS 2
>
> Timestamp: Tue Jan 4 11:25:09 2022, vdom root, health-check Test_MOS, interface: **port15**, status: up, latency: 0.097, jitter: 0.009, packet loss: 0.000%, **mos: 4.123**.
>
> Timestamp: Tue Jan 4 11:25:10 2022, vdom root, health-check Test_MOS, interface: **port15**, status: up, latency: 0.097, jitter: 0.008, packet loss: 0.000%, **mos: 4.123**.

Change the mos-codec to g722. The diagnostics will now display different MOS values:

diagnose sys sdwan health-check

Health Check(Test_MOS):

Seq(1 **dmz**): state(alive), packet-loss(0.000%) latency(0.150), jitter(0.031), **mos(4.453)**, bandwidth-up(999999), bandwidth-dw(999997), bandwidth-bi(1999996) sla_map=0x1

> Seq(2 **port15**): state(alive), packet-loss(0.000%) latency(0.104), jitter(0.008), **mos(4.453)**, bandwidth-up(999999), bandwidth-dw(999999), bandwidth-bi(1999998) sla_map=0x1

Increase the latency on the link in port15. The calculated MOS value will decrease accordingly. In this example, port15 is out of SLA since its MOS value is now less than the 4.0 minimum:

diagnose sys sdwan health-check

Health Check(Test_MOS):

Seq(1 dmz): state(alive), packet-loss(0.000%) latency(0.106), jitter(0.022), mos(4.453), bandwidth-up(999999), bandwidth-dw(999997), bandwidth-bi(1999996) sla_map=0x1

Seq(2 **port15**): state(alive), packet-loss(0.000%) latency(300.119), jitter(0.012), **mos(3.905)**, bandwidth-up(999999), bandwidth-dw(999999), bandwidth-bi(1999998) **sla_map=0x0**

Sample logs

date=2022-01-04 time=11:57:54 eventtime=1641326274876828300 tz="-0800" logid="0113022933" type="event" subtype="sdwan" level="notice" vd="root" logdesc="SDWAN SLA notification" eventtype="SLA" healthcheck="Test_MOS" slatargetid=1 **interface="port15"** status="up" latency="300.118" jitter="0.013" packetloss="0.000" **mos="3.905"** inbandwidthavailable="1000.00Mbps" outbandwidthavailable="1000.00Mbps" bibandwidthavailable="2.00Gbps" inbandwidthused="0kbps" outbandwidthused="0kbps" bibandwidthused="0kbps" **slamap="0x0"** metric="mos" msg="Health Check SLA status. **SLA failed due to being over the performance metric threshold.**"

date=2022-01-04 time=11:57:24 eventtime=1641326244286635920 tz="-0800" logid="0113022923" type="event" subtype="sdwan" level="notice" vd="root" logdesc="SDWAN status" eventtype="Health Check" healthcheck="Test_MOS" slatargetid=1 oldvalue="2" newvalue="1" msg="Number of pass member changed."

date=2022-01-04 time=11:57:24 eventtime=1641326244286627260 tz="-0800" logid="0113022923" type="event" subtype="sdwan" level="notice" vd="root" logdesc="SDWAN status" eventtype="Health Check" healthcheck="Test_MOS" slatargetid=1 member="2" msg="Member status changed. Member out-of-sla."

date=2022-01-04 time=11:57:02 eventtime=1641326222516756500 tz="-0800" logid="0113022925" type="event" subtype="sdwan" level="information" vd="root" logdesc="SDWAN SLA information" eventtype="SLA" healthcheck="Test_MOS" slatargetid=1 **interface="port15"** status="up" latency="0.106" jitter="0.007" packetloss="0.000" **mos="4.453"** inbandwidthavailable="1000.00Mbps" outbandwidthavailable="1000.00Mbps" bibandwidthavailable="2.00Gbps" inbandwidthused="0kbps" outbandwidthused="0kbps" bibandwidthused="0kbps" **slamap="0x1"** msg="Health Check SLA status."

SD-WAN rules

SD-WAN rules, which are sometimes called service rules, identify traffic of interest, and then route the traffic based on a strategy and the condition of the route or link between two devices. You can use many strategies to select the outgoing interface and many performance service level agreements (SLAs) to evaluate the link conditions.

Use the following topics to learn about and create SD-WAN rules for your needs:

- Overview
- Implicit rule
- Automatic strategy
- Manual strategy
- Best quality strategy
- Lowest cost (SLA) strategy
- Maximize bandwidth (SLA) strategy
- Use MAC addresses in SD-WAN rules and policy routes
- SD-WAN traffic shaping and QoS
- SDN dynamic connector addresses in SD-WAN rules
- Application steering using SD-WAN rules
- DSCP tag-based traffic steering in SD-WAN
- ECMP support for the longest match in SD-WAN rule matching
- Override quality comparisons in SD-WAN longest match rule matching
- Use an application category as an SD-WAN rule destination

Overview

SD-WAN rules control how sessions are distributed to SD-WAN members. You can configure SD-WAN rules from the GUI and CLI.

From the GUI, go to Network > SD-WAN > SD-WAN Rules. When creating a new SD-WAN rule, or editing an existing SD-WAN rule, use the Source and Destination sections to identify traffic, and use the Outgoing interfaces section to configure WAN intelligence for routing traffic.

From the CLI, use the following command to configure SD-WAN rules:

```
config system sdwan
    config service
        edit <ID>
        next
    end
end
```

The following topics describe the fields used to configure SD-WAN rules:

- Fields for identifying traffic
- Fields for configuring WAN intelligence
- Additional fields for configuring WAN intelligence

Fields for identifying traffic

This topic describes the fields in an SD-WAN rule used for defining the traffic to which the rule applies. Some fields are available only in the CLI.

SD-WAN rules can identify traffic by source address, destination address, service, and individual or user group matches. SD-WAN rules can also identify traffic by application control (application-aware routing), internet service database (ISDB), BGP route tags, and Differentiated Services Code Point (DSCP) tags.

In the GUI, go to Network > SD-WAN > SD-WAN Rules. Click Create New, or double-click an existing rule to open it for editing. The Source and Destination sections are used to identify traffic for the rule:

In the CLI, edit the service definition ID number to identify traffic for the rule:

config system sdwan

    config service

        edit <ID>

        <CLI commands from the following tables>

        ...

    end

end

The following table describes the fields used for the name, ID, and IP version of the SD-WAN rule:

Name, ID, and IP version		
Field	**CLI**	**Description**

Name, ID, and IP version		
Field	CLI	Description
Name	set name <string>	The name does not need to relate to the traffic being matched, but it is good practice to have intuitive rule names.
ID	config system sdwan config service **edit <ID>** next end end	ID is generated when the rule is created. You can only specify the ID from the CLI.
IP version	set addr-mode <ipv4 | ipv6>	The addressing mode can be IPv4 or IPv6. To configure in the GUI, IPv6 must be enabled from System > Feature Visibility page.

The following table describes the fields used for source section of the SD-WAN rule:

Source		
Field	CLI	Description
Source address	set src <object> May be negated from the CLI with set src-negate.	One or more address objects.
User group	set users <user object> set groups <group object>	Individual users or user groups

Source		
Field	**CLI**	**Description**
Source interface (input-device)	set input-device <interface name> May be negated with set input-device-negate enable.	CLI only. Select one or more source interfaces.

The following table describes the fields used for the destination section of the SD-WAN rule:

Destination		
Field	**CLI**	**Description**
Address	set dst <object> set protocol <integer> set start-port <integer>, set end-port <integer> Use set dst-negate enable to negate the address object.	One or more address objects. One protocol and one port range can be combined with the address object. If it is necessary for an SD-WAN rule to match multiple protocols or multiple port ranges, you can create a custom Internet Service.
Internet Service	set internet-service enable set internet-service-custom <name_1> <name_2> ... <name_n> set internet-service-custom-group <name_1> <name_2> ... <name_n> set internet-	One or more internet services or service groups. This applies only to IPv4 rules, and cannot be used in conjunction with an address object.

Destination		
Field	CLI	Description
	service-name <name_1> <name_2> ... <name_n> set internet-service-group <name_1> <name_2> ... <name_n>	
Application	set internet-service-app-ctrl <id_1> <id_2> ... <id_n> set internet-service-app-ctrl-group <name_1> <name_2> ... <name_n> set internet-service-app-ctrl-category <id_1> <id_2> ... <id_n>	One or more applications or application groups. This applies only to IPv4 rules, and cannot be used in conjunction with an address object. May be used with internet services or service group.
Route tag (route-tag)	set route-tag <integer>	CLI only. This replaces the dst field (if previously configured) and matches a BGP route tag configured in a route map.
TOS mask (tos-mask)	set tos-mask <8-bit hex value>	CLI only. In order to leverage type of service (TOS) matching or DSCP matching on the IP header, the SD-WAN rule must specify the bit mask of the byte holding the TOS value. For example, a TOS mask of 0xe0 (11100000) matches the upper 3 bits.

Destination		
Field	**CLI**	**Description**
TOS (tos)	set tos <8 bit hex value>	CLI only.
		The value specified here is matched after the tos-mask is applied.
		For example, the FortiGate receives DSCP values 110000 and 111011. (DSCP is the upper 6 bits of the TOS field – 11000000 and 11101100 respectively). Using the TOS value 0xe0 (11100000), only the second DSCP value is matched.

Fields for configuring WAN intelligence

This topic describes the fields in an SD-WAN rule used for configuring WAN intelligence, which processes and routes traffic that matches the SD-WAN rule.

In the GUI, go to Network > SD-WAN > SD-WAN Rules. Click Create New, or double-click an existing rule to open it for editing. The Outgoing Interfaces section is used to configure WAN intelligence for the rule:

WAN intelligence is comprised of the following parts:

- Interface or zone preference
- Strategy
- Performance SLA

Interface or zone preference

By default, the configured order of interfaces and/or zones in a rule are used. Interfaces and zones that are selected first have precedence over interfaces selected second and so on.

You can specify both interfaces and zones. When a zone is specified in the Zone preference field, it is equivalent to selecting each of the contained interface members in the Interface preference section. Interface members in a zone have lower priority than interfaces configured in the Interface preference section.

For example:

- There are 3 interfaces: port1, port2 and port3.
    - Port2 is in Zone1

- Port1 and port3 belong to the default virtual-wan-link zone.

- An SD-WAN rule is created with Interface preference set to port3 and port1, and Zone preference set to Zone1.

The SD-WAN rule prefers the interfaces in the following order:

1. port3

2. port1

3. port2

You can configure the interface and zone preference in the CLI:

```
config system sdwan
  config service
    edit <ID>
      set priority-members <integer>
      set priority-zone <interface>
    next
  end
end
```

Strategy

Strategy dictates how the interface and/or zone order changes as link conditions change. You can use the following strategies:

- Automatic (auto): interfaces are assigned a priority based on quality.

- Manual (manual): interfaces are manually assigned a priority.

- Best Quality (priority): interfaces are assigned a priority based on the link-cost-factor of the interface.

- Lowest cost (SLA) (sla): interfaces are assigned a priority based on selected SLA settings.

- Maximize Bandwidth (SLA) (load-balance): traffic is distributed among all available links based on the selected load balancing algorithm.

Performance SLA

The best quality, lowest cost, and maximize bandwidth strategies are the most intelligent modes, and they leverage SLA health checks to provide meaningful metrics for a given link. FortiGate uses the metrics to make intelligent decisions to route traffic.

Automatic and manual strategies have pre-configured logic that do not leverage SLA health checks.

The goal of the performance SLA is to measure the quality of each SD-WAN member link. The following methods can be used to measure the quality of a link:

- Active measurement

  - Health-check traffic is sent to a server with a variety of protocols options.

  - The following SLA metrics are measured on this probe traffic:

    - Latency

    - Jitter

    - Packet loss

- Passive measurement

  - SLA metrics are measured on real or live traffic, reducing the amount of probe traffic that is sent and received.

  - There is the option (prefer passive) to initiate probe traffic when no live traffic is present.

Performance SLA is utilized by auto, Lowest Cost (SLA), Maximize Bandwidth (SLA), and Best Quality strategies. Lowest Cost (SLA) and Maximize Bandwidth SLA use SLA targets in a pass or fail style to evaluate whether a link is considered for traffic. Best Quality compares a specific metric of the SLA to pick the best result.

Therefore it is integral to select or create an SLA target(s) that relates to the traffic targeted by the rule. It does not make sense to evaluate a public resource, such as YouTube, when the rule matches Azure traffic.

SD-WAN rules define specific policy routing options to route traffic to an SD-WAN member. When no explicit SD-WAN rules are defined, or if none of the rules are matched, then the default implicit rule is used.

Additional fields for configuring WAN intelligence

This topic describes the fields in an SD-WAN rule used for configuring WAN intelligence for egress traffic:

- Forward and/or reverse differentiated services code point (DSCP)
- Default and gateway options

For information about accessing fields for configuring WAN intelligence.

Forward and/or reverse differentiated services code point (DSCP)

The FortiGate differentiated services feature can be used to change the DSCP value for all packets accepted by a policy.

The packet's DSCP field for traffic initiating a session (forward) or for reply traffic (reverse) can be changed and enabled in each direction separately by configuring it in the firewall policy using the Forward DSCP and Reverse DSCP fields.

From the CLI:

```
config system sdwan
    config service
        edit <ID>
            ...
            set dscp-forward enable
            ...
        next
    end
end
```

set dscp-forward enable	Enable use of forward DSCP tag.
set dscp-forward-tag 000000	Forward traffic DSCP tag.

set dscp-reverse enable	Enable use of reverse DSCP tag.
set dscp-reverse-tag 000000	Reverse traffic DSCP tag.

Default and gateway options

Following are additional gateway options that can be set only in the CLI:

```
config system sdwan
    config service
        edit <ID>
            ...
            set default enable
            ...
        next
    end
end
```

set default [enable|disable]	Enable or disable use of SD-WAN as default service.
set gateway [enable|disable]	Enable or disable SD-WAN service gateway.

By default, these settings are set to disable.

These two commands help adjust FortiGate route selection by affecting how the FortiGate consults the Forward Information Base (FIB).

In order to decide whether an SD-WAN policy-route can be matched, FortiGate performs the following FIB lookups:

- FIB best match for the destination must return an SD-WAN member.

- FIB route to the destination must exist over the desired SD-WAN member.

When set default enable is used with set gateway enable, FortiGate bypasses the FIB checks, and instead routes any matching traffic of the

SD-WAN rule to the chosen SD-WAN member using the member's configured gateway. SD-WAN members must have a gateway configured.

When set default disable is used with set gateway enable, FortiGate keeps the first rule in effect but causes the second rule to change to:

- FIB route to the gateway IP address must exist over any interface.

Implicit rule

SD-WAN rules define specific policy routing options to route traffic to an SD-WAN member. When no explicit SD-WAN rules are defined, or if none of the rules are matched, then the default implicit rule is used.

In an SD-WAN configuration, the default route usually points to the SD-WAN interface, so each active member's gateway is added to the routing table's default route. FortiOS uses equal-cost multipath (ECMP) to balance traffic between the interfaces. One of five load balancing algorithms can be selected:

Source IP (source-ip-based)	Traffic is divided equally between the interfaces, including the SD-WAN interface. Sessions that start at the same source IP address use the same path.
	This is the default selection.
Sessions (weight-based)	The workload is distributing based on the number of sessions that are connected through the interface.
	The weight that you assign to each interface is used to calculate the percentage of the total sessions that are allowed to connect through an interface, and the sessions are distributed to the interfaces accordingly.
	Sessions with the same source and destination IP addresses (src-ip and dst-ip) are forwarded to the same path, but are still considered in later session ratio calculations.
	An interface's weight value cannot be zero.
Spillover (usage-based)	The interface is used until the traffic bandwidth exceeds the ingress and egress thresholds that you set for that interface. Additional traffic is then sent through the next SD-WAN interface member.
Source-Destination IP (source-dest-ip-based)	Traffic is divided equally between the interfaces. Sessions that start at the same source IP address and go to the same destination IP address use the same path.
Volume	The workload is distributing based on the number

(measured-volume-based)	of packets that are going through the interface.
	The volume weight that you assign to each interface is used to calculate the percentage of the total bandwidth that is allowed to go through an interface, and the bandwidth is distributed to the interfaces accordingly.
	An interface's volume value cannot be zero.

You cannot exclude an interface from participating in load balancing using the implicit rule. If the weight or volume were set to zero in a previous FortiOS version, the value is treated as a one.

Interfaces with static routes can be excluded from ECMP if they are configured with a lower priority than other static routes.

Examples

The following four examples demonstrate how to use the implicit rules (load-balance mode).

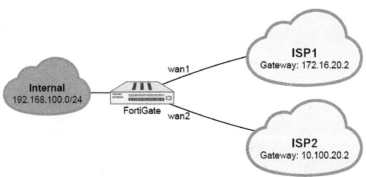

If no SD-WAN zone is specified, members are added to the default virtual-wan-link zone.

Example 1

Outgoing traffic is equally balanced between wan1 and wan2, using source-ip-based or source-dest-ip-based mode.

Using the GUI:

1. On the FortiGate, enable SD-WAN and add wan1 and wan2 as SD-WAN members, then add a policy and static route.

2. Go to Network > SD-WAN and select the SD-WAN Rules tab.

3. Edit the sd-wan rule (the last default rule).

4. For the Load Balancing Algorithm, select either Source IP or Source-Destination IP.

5. Click OK.

Using the CLI:

1. Enable SD-WAN and add wan1 and wan2 as SD-WAN members, then add a policy and static route.

2. Set the load balancing algorithm:

Source IP based:

```
config system sdwan
    set load-balance-mode source-ip-based
end
```

Source-Destination IP based:

```
config system sdwan
    set load-balance-mode source-dest-ip-based
end
```

Example 2

Outgoing traffic is balanced between wan1 and wan2 with a customized ratio, using weight-based mode: wan1 runs 80% of the sessions, and wan2 runs 20% of the sessions.

Sessions with the same source and destination IP addresses (src-ip and dst-ip) will be forwarded to the same path, but will still be considered in later session ratio calculations.

Using the GUI:

1. Go to Network > SD-WAN and select the SD-WAN Rules tab.

2. Edit the sd-wan rule (the last default rule).

3. For the Load Balancing Algorithm, select Sessions.

4. Enter 80 in the wan1 field, and 20 in the wan2 field.

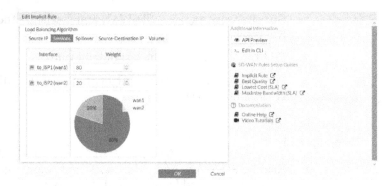

5. Click OK.

Using the CLI:

```
config system sdwan
    set load-balance-mode weight-based
    config members
        edit 1
            set interface "wan1"
            set weight 80
        next
        edit 2
            set interface "wan2"
            set weight 20
        next
    end
end
```

Example 3

Outgoing traffic is balanced between wan1 and wan2 with a customized ratio, using measured-volume-based mode: wan1 runs 80% of the volume, and wan2 runs 20% of the volume.

Using the GUI:

1. Go to Network > SD-WAN and select the SD-WAN Rules tab.

2. Edit the sd-wan rule (the last default rule).

3. For the Load Balancing Algorithm, select Volume.

4. Enter 80 in the wan1 field, and 20 in the wan2 field.

5. Click OK.

Using the CLI:

```
config system sdwan
    set load-balance-mode measured-volume-based
    config members
        edit 1
            set interface "wan1"
            set volume-ratio 80
        next
        edit 2
            set interface "wan2"
            set volume-ratio 20
        next
    end
end
```

Example 4

Load balancing can be used to reduce costs when internet connections are charged at different rates. For example, if wan2 charges based on volume usage and wan1 charges a fixed monthly fee, we can use wan1 at its maximum bandwidth, and use wan2 for overflow.

In this example, wan1's bandwidth is 10Mbps down and 2Mbps up. Traffic will use wan1 until it reaches its spillover limit, then it will start to use wan2. Note that auto-asic-offload must be disabled in the firewall policy.

Using the GUI:

1. On the FortiGate, enable SD-WAN and add wan1 and wan2 as SD-WAN members, then add a policy and static route.

2. Go to Network > SD-WAN and select the SD-WAN Rules tab.

3. Edit the sd-wan rule (the last default rule).

4. For the Load Balancing Algorithm, select Spillover.

5. Enter 10000 in the wan1 Ingress Spillover Threshold field, and 2000 in the wan1 Egress Spillover Threshold field.

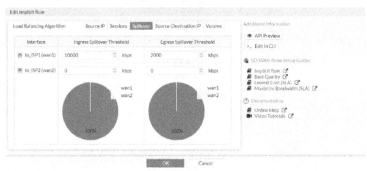

6. Click OK.

Using the CLI:

```
config system sdwan
    set load-balance-mode usage-based
    config members
        edit 1
            set interface "wan1"
            set spillover-threshold 2000
            set ingress-spillover-threshold 10000
        next
    end
end
```

Automatic strategy

The automatic strategy is a legacy rule that lets you select an outgoing interface based on its performance ranking compared to the other SD-WAN interfaces. This is achieved by applying a performance SLA to rank the interfaces, and then selecting the desired rank.

In this example, you have three SD-WAN interfaces to three different ISPs that all go to the public internet. WAN1 is your highest quality link and should be reserved for business critical traffic. WAN2 and WAN3 are redundant backup links. You noticed one non-critical application is taking up a lot of bandwidth and want to prioritize it to the lowest quality link at any given time.

To configure automatic SD-WAN rules from the CLI:

```
config system sdwan
  config members
    edit 1
      set interface "wan1"
    next
    edit 2
      set interface "wan2"
    next
    edit 3
      set interface "wan3"
    next
  end
  config health-check
    edit "non-critical application"
      set server "noncritical.application.com"
      set members 1 2 3
      config sla
        edit 1
          set latency-threshold 250
          set jitter-threshold 50
```

```
                set packletloss-threshold 3
            next
          end
       next
     end
   config service
     edit 1
        set name "non-critical application"
        set mode auto
        set quality-link 3
        set dst "non-critical-app-address-object"
        set health-check "non-critical application"
     next
   end
end
```

The auto option is only available in the CLI. If you use the GUI to edit the rule, the auto option will be overwritten because you cannot select auto in the GUI.

Manual strategy

In manual mode, no health checks are used. As a result, the decision making closer resembles logic than intelligence. SD-WAN manual rules are similar to regular policy-based routes, but have the added features of application-aware routing and BGP-tag routing. A manual strategy rule is comprised of the following parts:

- Defining the interfaces to be used
- Ordering the interfaces based on preference

To configure manual SD-WAN rules from the GUI:

1. Go to Network > SD-WAN.
2. Select the SD-WAN Rules tab, and click Create New.
3. Set the following options to create a manual rule:

Name	Type a name for the rule.
Source	(Optional) Specify a Source address and/or User group.
Destination	Specify the destination using an Address object or an Internet Service or an Application.
Zone preference	Specify one or more SD-WAN interfaces or zones. The order in which the interfaces or zones are specified determines their priority when the rule is matched.

4. Set the remaining options as desired, and click OK to create the rule.

To configure manual SD-WAN rules from the CLI:

config system sdwan

```
config members
    edit 1
        set interface "wan1"
    next
    edit 2
        set interface "wan2"
    next
end
config service
    edit 1
        set name "manual"
        set mode manual
        set priority-members 2 1
        set dst "DC_net"
        set hold-down-time 60
    next
end
end
```

- The command set mode manual will not appear in the configuration because it is the default mode.
- The command set hold-down-time <integer> is an optional command that controls how long to wait before switching back to the primary interface in the event of a failover.

Best quality strategy

When using Best Quality mode, SD-WAN will choose the best link to forward traffic by comparing the link-cost-factor. A link-cost factor is a specific metric of participating link(s) (such as, latency, packet loss, and so on) evaluated against a target that you define (such as a health-check server), for example, the latency of WAN1 and WAN2 to your datacenter. Below is a list of link-cost factors available to you:

GUI	CLI	Description
Latency	latency	Select a link based on latency.
Jitter	jitter	Select a link based on jitter.
Packet Loss	packet-loss	Select a link based on packet loss.
Downstream	inbandwidth	Select a link based on available bandwidth of incoming traffic.
Upstream	outbandwidth	Select a link based on available bandwidth of outgoing traffic.
Bandwidth	bibandwidth	Select a link based on available bandwidth of bidirectional traffic.
Customized profile	custom-profile-1	Select link based on customized profile. If selected, set the following weights: • packet-loss-weight: Coefficient of packet-loss. • latency-weight: Coefficient of latency. • jitter-weight: Coefficient of jitter. • bandwidth-weight: Coefficient of reciprocal of available bidirectional bandwidth.

Although SD-WAN intelligence selects the best quality link according to the selected metric, by default a preference or advantage is given to the first configured SD-WAN member. This default is 10% and may be configured with the CLI command set link-cost-threshold 10.

Example of how link-cost-threshold works:

```
config system sdwan
    config members
        edit 1
            set interface "wan1"
        next
        edit 2
            set interface "wan2"
        next
    end
    config service
        edit 1
            set name "Best_Quality"
            set mode priority
            set priority-members 2 1
            set dst "DC_net"
            set health-check "DC_HealthCheck"
            set link-cost-factor latency
            set link-cost-threshold 10
        next
    end
end
```

In this example both WAN1 and WAN2 are assumed to have 200ms latency to the health-check server named DC_HealthCheck. Because WAN2 is specified before WAN1 in priority-members, SD-WAN parses the two interfaces metric as follows:

- WAN1: 200ms

- WAN2: 200ms / (1+10%) = ~182ms

As a result, WAN2 is selected because the latency is lower.

If the Downstream (inbandwidth), Upstream (outbandwidth), or Bandwidth (bibandwidth) quality criteria is used, the FortiGate uses the upstream and downstream bandwidth values configured on the member interfaces to calculate bandwidth.

The interface bandwidth configuration can be done manually, or the interface speedtest can be used to populate the bandwidth values based on the speedtest results. See Manual interface speedtest for details.

To manually configure the upstream and downstream interface bandwidth values:

config system interface

    edit <interface>

        set estimated-upstream-bandwidth <speed in kbps>

        set estimated-downstream-bandwidth <speed in kbps>

    next

end

Example

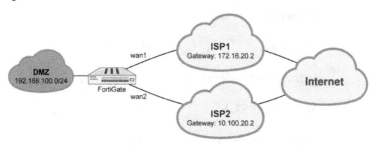

In this example, your wan1 and wan2 SD-WAN interfaces connect to two ISPs that both go to the public internet, and you want Gmail services to use the link with the least latency.

To configure an SD-WAN rule to use Best Quality:

1. On the FortiGate, add wan1 and wan2 as SD-WAN members, then add a policy and static route.

2. Create a new Performance SLA named google.

3. Go to Network > SD-WAN, select the SD-WAN Rules tab, and click Create New.

4. Enter a name for the rule, such as gmail.

5. Configure the following settings:

Internet Service	Google-Gmail
Strategy	Best Quality
Interface preference	wan1 and wan2
Measured SLA	google (created in step 2).
Quality criteria	Latency

6. Click OK to create the rule.

To configure an SD-WAN rule to use priority:

```
config system sdwan
    config health-check
        edit "google"
```

```
        set server "google.com"
        set members 1 2
    next
  end
  config service
    edit 1
        set name "gmail"
        set mode priority
        set internet-service enable
        set internet-service-id 65646
        set health-check "google"
        set link-cost-factor latency
        set priority-members 1 2
    next
  end
end
```

To diagnose the Performance SLA status:

FGT # diagnose sys sdwan health-check google

Health Check(google):

Seq(1): state(alive), packet-loss(0.000%) latency(14.563), jitter(4.334) sla_map=0x0

Seq(2): state(alive), packet-loss(0.000%) latency(12.633), jitter(6.265) sla_map=0x0

FGT # diagnose sys sdwan service 1

Service(1):

TOS(0x0/0x0), protocol(0: 1->65535), Mode(priority), link-cost-facotr(latency), link-cost-threshold(10), health-check(google) Members:

1: Seq_num(2), alive, latency: 12.633, selected

2: Seq_num(1), alive, latency: 14.563, selected

Internet Service: Google-Gmail(65646)

As wan2 has a smaller latency, SD-WAN will put Seq_num(2) on top of Seq_num(1) and wan2 will be used to forward Gmail traffic.

Lowest cost (SLA) strategy

When using Lowest Cost (SLA) mode (sla in the CLI), SD-WAN will choose the lowest cost link that satisfies SLA to forward traffic. The lowest possible cost is 0. If multiple eligible links have the same cost, the Interface preference order will be used to select a link.

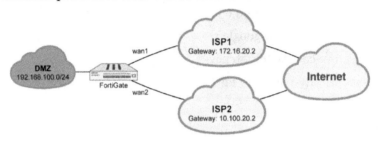

In this example, your wan1 and wan2 SD-WAN interfaces connect to two ISPs that both go to the public internet. The cost of wan2 is less than that of wan1. You want to configure Gmail services to use the lowest cost interface, but the link quality must meet a standard of latency: 10ms, and jitter: 5ms.

To configure an SD-WAN rule to use Lowest Cost (SLA):

1. On the FortiGate, add wan1 and wan2 as SD-WAN members, then add a policy and static route.

2. Create a new Performance SLA named google that includes an SLA Target with Latency threshold = 10ms and Jitter threshold = 5ms.

3. Go to Network > SD-WAN, select the SD-WAN Rules tab, and click Create New.

4. Enter a name for the rule, such as gmail.

5. Configure the following settings:

Internet Service	Google-Gmail
Strategy	Lowest Cost (SLA)
Interface preference	wan1 and wan2
Required SLA target	google (created in step 2).

6. Click OK to create the rule.

To configure an SD-WAN rule to use SLA:

```
config system sdwan
  config members
    edit 1
      set interface "wan1"
      set cost 10
    next
```

```
        edit 2
            set interface "wan2"
            set cost 5
        next
    end
    config health-check
        edit "google"
            set server "google.com"
            set members 1 2
            config sla
                edit 1
                    set latency-threshold 10
                    set jitter-threshold 5
                next
            end
        next
    end
    config service
        edit 1
            set name "gmail"
            set mode sla
            set internet-service enable
            set internet-service-id 65646
            config sla
                edit "google"
                    set id 1
                next
            end
            set priority-members 1 2
        next
    end
```

end

If no SD-WAN zone is specified, members are added to the default virtual-wan-link zone.

The CLI command set minimum-sla-meet-members allows you to specify the number of links that must meet SLA for the rule to take effect. If the number of members is less than the minimum set with this command, the rule will not take effect.

To diagnose the Performance SLA status:

FGT # **diagnose sys sdwan health-check google**

Health Check(google):

Seq(1): state(alive), packet-loss(0.000%) latency(14.563), jitter(4.334) sla_map=0x0

Seq(2): state(alive), packet-loss(0.000%) latency(12.633), jitter(6.265) sla_map=0x0

FGT # **diagnose sys sdwan service 1**

Service(1): Address Mode(IPV4) flags=0x0

TOS(0x0/0x0), Protocol(0: 1->65535), Mode(sla)

Members:<
>

1: Seq_num(2), alive, sla(0x1), cfg_order(1), selected

2: Seq_num(1), alive, sla(0x1), cfg_order(0), selected

Internet Service: Google.Gmail(65646)

When both wan1 and wan2 meet the SLA requirements, Gmail traffic will only use wan2. If only wan1 meets the SLA requirements, Gmail traffic will only use wan1, even though it has a higher cost. If neither interface meets the requirements, wan2 will be used.

If both interface had the same cost and both met the SLA requirements, the first link configured in set priority-members would be used.

Maximize bandwidth (SLA) strategy

When using Maximize Bandwidth mode (load-balance in the CLI), SD-WAN will choose all of the links that satisfies SLA to forward traffic based on a load balancing algorithm. The load balancing algorithm, or hash method, can be one of the following:

round-robin   All traffic are distributed to selected interfaces in equal portions and circular order.

                   This is the default method, and the only option available when using the GUI.

source-ip-based   All traffic from a source IP is sent to the same interface.

source-dest-ip-based   All traffic from a source IP to a destination IP is sent to the same interface.

inbandwidth   All traffic are distributed to a selected interface with most available bandwidth for incoming traffic.

outbandwidth   All traffic are distributed to a selected interface with most available bandwidth for outgoing traffic.

bibandwidth   All traffic are distributed to a selected interface with most available bandwidth for both incoming and outgoing traffic.

When the inbandwidth, outbandwidth), or bibandwidth load balancing algorithm is used, the FortiGate will compare the bandwidth based on the configured upstream and downstream bandwidth values.

The interface speedtest can be used to populate the bandwidth values based on the speedtest results.

To manually configure the upstream and downstream bandwidth values:

config system interface

    edit <interface>

       set estimated-upstream-bandwidth <speed in kbps>

       set estimated-downstream-bandwidth <speed in kbps>

    next

end

ADVPN is not supported in this mode.

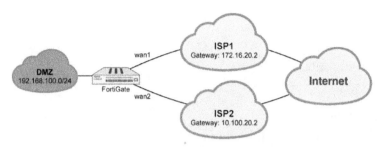

In this example, your wan1 and wan2 SD-WAN interfaces connect to two ISPs that both go to the public internet. You want to configure Gmail services to use both of the interface, but the link quality must meet a standard of latency: 10ms, and jitter: 5ms. This can maximize the bandwidth usage.

To configure an SD-WAN rule to use Maximize Bandwidth (SLA):

1. On the FortiGate, add wan1 and wan2 as SD-WAN members, then add a policy and static route.

2. Create a new Performance SLA named google that includes an SLA Target 1 with Latency threshold = 10ms and Jitter threshold = 5ms.

3. Go to Network > SD-WAN, select the SD-WAN Rules tab, and click Create New.

4. Enter a name for the rule, such as gmail.

5. Configure the following settings:

Field	Setting
Internet Service	Google-Gmail
Strategy	Maximize Bandwidth (SLA)
Interface preference	wan1 and wan2
Required SLA target	google (created in step 2).

6. Click OK to create the rule.

To configure an SD-WAN rule to use SLA:

```
config system sdwan
    config health-check
        edit "google"
            set server "google.com"
            set members 1 2
            config sla
                edit 1
                    set latency-threshold 10
                    set jitter-threshold 5
                next
            end
        next
    end
    config service
        edit 1
            set name "gmail"
            set addr-mode ipv4
            set mode load-balance
            set hash-mode round-robin
            set internet-service enable
            set internet-service-name Google-Gmail
            config sla
                edit "google"
                    set id 1
                next
            end
            set priority-members 1 2
        next
    end
end
```

The CLI command set minimum-sla-meet-members allows you to specify the number of links that must meet SLA for the rule to take effect. If the number of members is less than the minimum set with this command, the rule will not take effect.

To diagnose the performance SLA status:

FGT # **diagnose sys sdwan health-check google**

Health Check(google):

Seq(1): state(alive), packet-loss(0.000%) latency(14.563), jitter(4.334) sla_map=0x0

Seq(2): state(alive), packet-loss(0.000%) latency(12.633), jitter(6.265) sla_map=0x0

FGT # **diagnose sys sdwan service 1**

Service(1): Address Mode(IPV4) flags=0x0

TOS(0x0/0x0), Protocol(0: 1->65535), Mode(load-balance)

Members:<
>

1: Seq_num(1), alive, sla(0x1), num of pass(1), selected

2: Seq_num(2), alive, sla(0x1), num of pass(1), selected

Internet Service: Google.Gmail(65646)

When both wan1 and wan2 meet the SLA requirements, Gmail traffic will use both wan1 and wan2. If only one of the interfaces meets the SLA requirements, Gmail traffic will only use that interface.

If neither interface meets the requirements but health-check is still alive, then wan1 and wan2 tie. The traffic will try to balance between wan1 and wan2, using both interfaces to forward traffic.

Use MAC addresses in SD-WAN rules and policy routes

You can use MAC addresses as the source in SD-WAN rules and policy routes.

The FABRIC_DEVICE address object (a dynamic object that includes the IPs of Security Fabric devices) can be used as a source or destination in SD-WAN rules and policy routes.

The diagnose ip proute match command accepts either the IP or MAC address format for the source:

diagnose ip proute match <destination> <source> <interface> <protocol> <port>

To configure a MAC address as a source for SD-WAN and a policy route:

Configure the MAC address:

```
config firewall address
    edit "mac-add"
        set type mac
        set macaddr 70:4c:a5:86:de:56
    next
            end
```

Configure the policy route:

```
config router policy
    edit 3
        set srcaddr "mac-add"
        set gateway 15.1.1.34
        set output-device ha
    next
            end
```

Configure the SD-WAN rule:

```
config system sdwan
    config service
        edit 1
```

```
        set dst "all"
        set src "mac-add"
        set priority-members 1
    next
    edit 2
        set dst "FABRIC_DEVICE"
        set priority-members 2
    next
end
        end
```

To verify the policy route matching for a MAC address:

```
# diagnose ip proute match 3.1.1.34 70:4c:a5:86:de:56 port3 22 6
dst=3.1.1.34  src=0.0.0.0  smac=70:4c:a5:86:de:56  iif=11  protocol=22
dport=6
id=00000003 type=Policy Route
seq-num=3
```

SD-WAN traffic shaping and QoS

Use a traffic shaper in a firewall shaping policy to control traffic flow. You can use it to control maximum and guaranteed bandwidth, or put certain traffic to one of the three different traffic priorities: high, medium, or low.

An advanced shaping policy can classify traffic into 30 groups. Use a shaping profile to define the percentage of the interface bandwidth that is allocated to each group. Each group of traffic is shaped to the assigned speed limit based on the outgoing bandwidth limit configured on the interface.

Sample topology

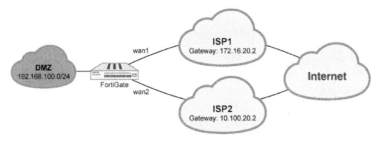

Sample configuration

This example shows a typical customer usage where the customer's SD-WAN uses the default zone, and has two member: wan1 and wan2, each set to 10Mb/s.

An overview of the procedures to configure SD-WAN traffic shaping and QoS with SD-WAN includes:

1. Give HTTP/HTTPS traffic high priority and give FTP low priority so that if there are conflicts, FortiGate will forward HTTP/HTTPS traffic first.

2. Even though FTP has low priority, configure FortiGate to give it a 1Mb/s guaranteed bandwidth on each SD-WAN member so that if there is no FTP traffic, other traffic can use all the bandwidth. If there is heavy FTP traffic, it can still be guaranteed a 1Mb/s bandwidth.

3. Traffic going to specific destinations such as a VOIP server uses wan1 to forward, and SD-WAN forwards with an Expedited Forwarding (EF) DSCP tag 101110.

To configure SD-WAN traffic shaping and QoS with SD-WAN in the GUI:

1. On the FortiGate, add wan1 and wan2 as SD-WAN members, then add a policy and static route.

2. Add a firewall policy with Application Control enabled.

3. Go to Policy & Objects > Traffic Shaping, select the Traffic Shapers tab, and edit low-priority.

    1. Enable Guaranteed Bandwidth and set it to 1000 kbps.

4. Go to Policy & Objects > Traffic Shaping, select the Traffic Shaping Policies tab, and click Create New.

    1. Name the traffic shaping policy, for example, HTTP-HTTPS.

    2. Set the following:

Source	all
Destination	all
Service	HTTP and HTTPS
Outgoing interface	virtual-wan-link
Shared Shaper	Enable and set to high-priority
Reverse Shaper	Enable and set to high-priority

    3. Click OK.

5. Go to Policy & Objects > Traffic Shaping, select the Traffic Shaping Policies tab, and click Create New.ss

    1. Name the traffic shaping policy, for example, FTP.

    2. Set the following:

Source	all
Destination	all

Service	FTP, FTP_GET, and FTP_PUT
Outgoing interface	virtual-wan-link
Shared Shaper	Enable and set to low-priority
Reverse Shaper	Enable and set to low-priority

    3. Click OK

6. Go to Network > SD-WAN, select the SD-WAN Rules tab, and click Create New.

    1. Enter a name for the rule, such as Internet.

    2. In the Destination section, click Address and select the VoIP server that you created in the firewall address.

    3. Under Outgoing Interfaces select Manual.

    4. For Interface preference select wan1.

    5. Click OK.

7. Use CLI commands to modify DSCP settings. See the DSCP CLI commands below.

To configure the firewall policy using the CLI:

```
config firewall policy
    edit 1
        set name "1"
        set srcintf "dmz"
        set dstintf "virtual-wan-link"
        set srcaddr "all"
        set dstaddr "all"
        set action accept
```

```
            set schedule "always"
            set service "ALL"
            set utm-status enable
            set ssl-ssh-profile "certificate-inspection"
            set application-list "default"
            set nat enable
        next
    end
```

To configure the firewall traffic shaper priority using the CLI:

```
config firewall shaper traffic-shaper
    edit "high-priority"
        set maximum-bandwidth 1048576
        set per-policy enable
    next
    edit "low-priority"
        set guaranteed-bandwidth 1000
        set maximum-bandwidth 1048576
        set priority low
        set per-policy enable
    next
end
```

To configure the firewall traffic shaping policy using the CLI:

```
config firewall shaping-policy
    edit 1
        set name "http-https"
        set service "HTTP" "HTTPS"
        set dstintf "virtual-wan-link"
```

```
        set traffic-shaper "high-priority"
        set traffic-shaper-reverse "high-priority"
        set srcaddr "all"
        set dstaddr "all"
    next
    edit 2
        set name "FTP"
        set service "FTP" "FTP_GET" "FTP_PUT"
        set dstintf "virtual-wan-link"
        set traffic-shaper "low-priority"
        set traffic-shaper-reverse "low-priority"
        set srcaddr "all"
        set dstaddr "all"
    next
end
```

To configure SD-WAN traffic shaping and QoS with SD-WAN in the CLI:

```
config system sdwan
    set status enable
    config members
        edit 1
            set interface "wan1"
            set gateway 172.16.20.2
        next
        edit 2
            set interface "wan2"
            set gateway 10.100.20.2
        next
    end
```

```
config service
    edit 1
        set name "SIP"
        set priority-members 1
        set dst "voip-server"
        set dscp-forward enable
        set dscp-forward-tag 101110
    next
    end
end
```

If no SD-WAN zone is specified, members are added to the default virtual-wan-link zone.

To use the diagnose command to check if specific traffic is attached to the correct traffic shaper:

diagnose firewall iprope list 100015

policy index=1 uuid_idx=0 action=accept

flag (0):

shapers: orig=high-priority(2/0/134217728)   reply=high-priority(2/0/134217728)

cos_fwd=0 cos_rev=0

group=00100015 av=00000000 au=00000000 split=00000000

host=0 chk_client_info=0x0 app_list=0 ips_view=0

misc=0 dd_type=0 dd_mode=0

zone(1): 0 -> zone(2): 36 38

source(1): 0.0.0.0-255.255.255.255, uuid_idx=6,

dest(1): 0.0.0.0-255.255.255.255, uuid_idx=6,

service(2):

    [6:0x0:0/(1,65535)->(80,80)] helper:auto

[6:0x0:0/(1,65535)->(443,443)] helper:auto

policy index=2 uuid_idx=0 action=accept

flag (0):

shapers: orig=low-priority(4/128000/134217728)   reply=low-priority(4/128000/134217728)

cos_fwd=0 cos_rev=0

group=00100015 av=00000000 au=00000000 split=00000000

host=0 chk_client_info=0x0 app_list=0 ips_view=0

misc=0 dd_type=0 dd_mode=0

zone(1): 0 -> zone(2): 36 38

source(1): 0.0.0.0-255.255.255.255, uuid_idx=6,

dest(1): 0.0.0.0-255.255.255.255, uuid_idx=6,

service(3):

    [6:0x0:0/(1,65535)->(21,21)] helper:auto

    [6:0x0:0/(1,65535)->(21,21)] helper:auto

    [6:0x0:0/(1,65535)->(21,21)] helper:auto

To use the diagnose command to check if the correct traffic shaper is applied to the session:

diagnose sys session list

session info: proto=6 proto_state=01 duration=11 expire=3599 timeout=3600 flags=00000000 sockflag=00000000 sockport=0 av_idx=0 use=5

origin-shaper=low-priority prio=4 guarantee 128000Bps max 1280000Bps traffic 1050Bps drops 0B

reply-shaper=

per_ip_shaper=

class_id=0 shaping_policy_id=2 ha_id=0 policy_dir=0 tunnel=/ helper=ftp vlan_cos=0/255

state=may_dirty npu npd os mif route_preserve

statistic(bytes/packets/allow_err): org=868/15/1 reply=752/10/1 tuples=2 tx speed(Bps/kbps): 76/0 rx speed(Bps/kbps): 66/0

orgin->sink: org pre->post, reply pre->post dev=39->38/38->39 gwy=172.16.200.55/0.0.0.0

hook=post   dir=org   act=snat   10.1.100.11:58241->172.16.200.55:21(172.16.200.1:58241)

hook=pre   dir=reply   act=dnat   172.16.200.55:21->172.16.200.1:58241(10.1.100.11:58241)

pos/(before,after) 0/(0,0), 0/(0,0)

misc=0 policy_id=1 auth_info=0 chk_client_info=0 vd=4

serial=0003255f tos=ff/ff app_list=0 app=0 url_cat=0

sdwan_mbr_seq=0 sdwan_service_id=0

rpdb_link_id = 00000000

dd_type=0 dd_mode=0

npu_state=0x100000

npu info: flag=0x00/0x00, offload=0/0, ips_offload=0/0, epid=0/0, ipid=0/0, vlan=0x0000/0x0000

vlifid=0/0, vtag_in=0x0000/0x0000 in_npu=0/0, out_npu=0/0, fwd_en=0/0, qid=0/0

no_ofld_reason: offload-denied helper

total session 1

To use the diagnose command to check the status of a shared traffic shaper:

diagnose firewall shaper traffic-shaper list

name high-priority

maximum-bandwidth 131072 KB/sec

guaranteed-bandwidth 0 KB/sec

current-bandwidth 0 B/sec

priority 2

tos ff

packets dropped 0

bytes dropped 0

name low-priority
maximum-bandwidth 131072 KB/sec
guaranteed-bandwidth 125 KB/sec
current-bandwidth 0 B/sec
priority 4
tos ff
packets dropped 0
bytes dropped 0

name high-priority
maximum-bandwidth 131072 KB/sec
guaranteed-bandwidth 0 KB/sec
current-bandwidth 0 B/sec
priority 2
policy 1
tos ff
packets dropped 0
bytes dropped 0

name low-priority
maximum-bandwidth 131072 KB/sec
guaranteed-bandwidth 125 KB/sec
current-bandwidth 0 B/sec
priority 4
policy 2
tos ff
packets dropped 0
bytes dropped 0

SDN dynamic connector addresses in SD-WAN rules

SDN dynamic connector addresses can be used in SD-WAN rules. FortiGate supports both public (AWS, Azure, GCP, OCI, AliCloud) and private (Kubernetes, VMware ESXi and NSX, OpenStack, ACI, Nuage) SDN connectors.

The configuration procedure for all of the supported SDN connector types is the same. This example uses an Azure public SDN connector.

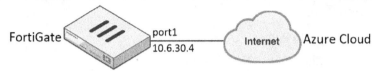

There are four steps to create and use an SDN connector address in an SD-WAN rule:

1. Configure the FortiGate IP address and network gateway so that it can reach the Internet.

2. Create an Azure SDN connector.

3. Create a firewall address to associate with the configured SDN connector.

4. Use the firewall address in an SD-WAN service rule.

To create an Azure SDN connector:

1. Go to Security Fabric > External Connectors.

2. Click Create New.

3. In the Public SDN section, click Microsoft Azure.

4. Enter the following:

Name	azure1
Status	Enabled
Update Interval	Use Default
Server region	Global
Directory ID	942b80cd-1b14-42a1-8dcf-4b21dece61ba
Application ID	14dbd5c5-307e-4ea4-8133-

68738141feb1

Client secret	xxxxxx
Resource path	disabled

5. Click OK.

To create a firewall address to associate with the configured SDN connector:

1. Go to Policy & Objects > Addresses.
2. Click Create New > Address.
3. Enter the following:

Category	Address
Name	azure-address
Type	Dynamic
Sub Type	Fabric Connector Address
SDN Connector	azure1
SDN address type	Private
Filter	SecurityGroup=edsouza-centos
Interface	Any

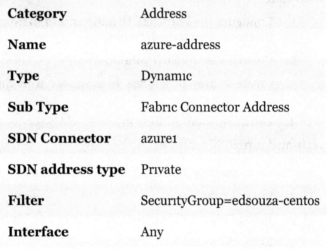

4. Click OK.

To use the firewall address in an SD-WAN service rule:

1. Go to Network > SD-WAN, select the SD-WAN Rules tab, and click Create New.
2. Set the Name to Azure1.
3. For the Destination Address select azure-address.
4. Configure the remaining settings as needed.
5. Click OK.

Diagnostics

Use the following CLI commands to check the status of and troubleshoot the connector.

To see the status of the SDN connector:

```
# diagnose sys sdn status
```

SDN Connector	Type	Status	Updating	Last update
azure1	azure	connected	no	n/a

To debug the SDN connector to resolve the firewall address:

```
# diagnose debug application azd -1
    Debug messages will be on for 30 minutes.


    ...

    azd sdn connector azure1 start updating IP addresses
    azd checking firewall address object azure-address-1, vd 0
    IP address change, new list:
    10.18.0.4
    10.18.0.12
    ...

    ...

# diagnose sys sdwan service
```

Service(2): Address Mode(IPV4) flags=0x0

TOS(0x0/0x0), Protocol(0: 1->65535), Mode(manual)

Service role: standalone

Member sub interface:

Members:

1: Seq_num(1), alive, selected

Dst address:

10.18.0.4 - 10.18.0.4

10.18.0.12 - 10.18.0.12

... ...

... ...

... ...

Application steering using SD-WAN rules

This topic covers how to use application steering in a topology with multiple WAN links. The following examples illustrate how to use different strategies to perform application steering to accommodate different business needs:

- Static application steering with a manual strategy
- Dynamic application steering with lowest cost and best quality strategies

Application matching

To apply application steering, SD-WAN service rules match traffic based on the applications that are in the application signature database. To view the signatures, go to Security Profiles > Application Signatures and select Signature.

On the first session that passes through, the IPS engine processes the traffic in the application layer to match it to a signature in the application signature database. The first session does not match any SD-WAN rules because the signature has not been recognized yet. When the IPS engine recognizes the application, it records the 3-tuple IP address, protocol, and port in the application control Internet Service ID list. To view the application and corresponding 3-tuple:

diagnose sys sdwan internet-service-app-ctrl-list [app ID]

52.114.142.254

Microsoft.Teams(43541 4294837333): 52.114.142.254 6 443 Fri Jun 18 13:52:18 2021

The recognized application and 3-tuple stay in the application control list for future matches to occur. If there are no hits on the entry for eight hours, the entry is deleted.

For services with multiple IP addresses, traffic might not match the expected SD-WAN rule because the traffic is destined for an IP address that hat no previously been recognized by the FortiGate. The diagnose sys sdwan internet-service-app-ctrl-list command can be used to help troubleshoot such situations.

Static application steering with a manual strategy

This example covers a typical usage scenario where the SD-WAN has two members: MPLS and DIA. DIA is primarily used for direct internet access to internet applications, such as Office365, Google applications, Amazon, and Dropbox. MPLS is primarily used for SIP, and works as a backup when DIA is not working.

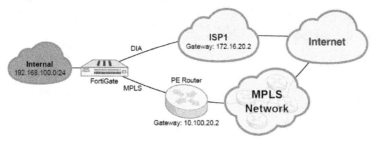

This example configures all SIP traffic to use MPLS while all other traffic uses DIA. If DIA is not working, the traffic will use MPLS.

To configure an SD-WAN rule to use SIP and DIA in the GUI:

1. Add port1 (DIA) and port2 (MPLS) as SD-WAN members, and configure a static route.

2. Create a firewall policy with an Application Control profile configured.

3. Go to Network > SD-WAN, select the SD-WAN Rules tab, and click Create New.

4. Enter a name for the rule, such as SIP.

5. Click the Application field and select the applicable SIP applications from the Select Entries panel.

6. Under Outgoing Interfaces, select Manual.

7. For Interface preference, select MPLS.

8. Click OK.

9. Click Create New to create another rule.

10. Enter a name for the rule, such as Internet.

11. Click the Address field and select all from the panel.

12. Under Outgoing Interfaces, select Manual.

13. For Interface preference, select DIA.

14. Click OK.

To configure the firewall policy using the CLI:

```
config firewall policy
    edit 1
        set name "1"
        set srcintf "dmz"
        set dstintf "virtual-wan-link"
        set srcaddr "all"
        set dstaddr "all"
        set action accept
        set schedule "always"
        set service "ALL"
        set utm-status enable
        set fsso disable
        set application-list "default"
        set ssl-ssh-profile "certificate-inspection"
        set nat enable
    next
end
```

To configure an SD-WAN rule to use SIP and DIA using the CLI:

```
config system sdwan
    set status enable
    config members
        edit 1
            set interface "MPLS"
        next
        edit 2
            set interface "DIA"
        next
    end
```

```
config service
    edit 1
        set name "SIP"
        set internet-service enable
        set internet-service-app-ctrl 34640 152305677 38938 26180 26179
30251
        set priority-members 2
    next
    edit 2
        set name "Internet"
        set dst "all"
        set priority-members 1
    next
  end
end
```

All SIP traffic uses MPLS. All other traffic goes to DIA. If DIA is broken, the traffic uses MPLS. If you use VPN instead of MPLS to run SIP traffic, you must configure a VPN interface, for example vpn1, and then replace member 1 from MPLS to vpn1 for SD-WAN member.

If no SD-WAN zone is specified, members are added to the default virtual-wan-link zone.

To use the diagnose command to check performance SLA status using the CLI:

diagnose sys sdwan service 1

Service(1): Address Mode(IPV4) flags=0x0

TOS(0x0/0x0), Protocol(0: 1->65535), Mode(manual)
Members:<
>

153

1: Seq_num(1), alive, selected

Internet Service: SIP(4294836224 34640) SIP.Method(4294836225 152305677) SIP.Via.NAT(4294836226 38938) SIP_Media.Type.Application(4294836227 26180) SIP_Message(4294836228 26179) SIP_Voice(4294836229 30251)

diagnose sys sdwan service 2

Service(2): Address Mode(IPV4) flags=0x0

TOS(0x0/0x0), Protocol(0: 1->65535), Mode(manual)

Members:<
>

1: Seq_num(2), alive, selected

Dst address: 0.0.0.0-255.255.255.255

diagnose sys sdwan internet-service-app-ctrl-list

Ctrl application(SIP 34640):Internet Service ID(4294836224)

Ctrl application(SIP.Method 152305677):Internet Service ID(4294836225)

Ctrl application(SIP.Via.NAT 38938):Internet Service ID(4294836226)

Ctrl application(SIP_Media.Type.Application 26180):Internet Service ID(4294836227)

Ctrl application(SIP_Message 26179):Internet Service ID(4294836228)

Ctrl application(SIP_Voice 30251):Internet Service ID(4294836229)

Dynamic application steering with lowest cost and best quality strategies

In this example, the SD-WAN has three members: two ISPs (DIA_1 and DIA_2) that are used for access to internet applications, and an MPLS link that is used exclusively as a backup for business critical applications.

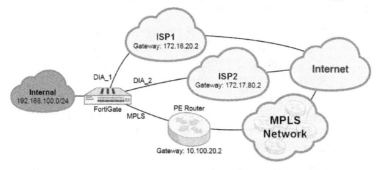

Business applications, such as Office365, Google, Dropbox, and SIP, use the Lowest Cost (SLA) strategy to provide application steering, and traffic falls back to MPLS only if both ISP1 and ISP2 are down. Non-business applications, such as Facebook and Youtube, use the Best Quality strategy to choose between the ISPs.

To configure the SD-WAN members, static route, and firewall policy in the GUI:

1. Add port1 (DIA_1), port2 (DIA_2), and port3 (MPLS) as SD-WAN members. Set the cost of DIA_1 and DIA_2 to 0, and MPLS to 20.

2. Configure a static route.

3. Create a firewall policy to allow traffic out on SD-WAN, with an Application Control profile configured.

To configure the SD-WAN rule and performance SLA checks for business critical application in the GUI:

1. Go to Network > SD-WAN, select the SD-WAN Rules tab, and click Create New.

2. Set the name to BusinessCriticalApps.

   This rule will steer your business critical traffic to the appropriate link based on the Lowest Cost (SLA).

3. Set Source address to all.

4. Under Destination, set Application to your required applications. In this example: Microsoft.Office.365, Microsoft.Office.Online, Google.Docs, Dropbox, and SIP.

5. Under Outgoing Interfaces, select Lowest Cost (SLA).

   The lowest cost is defined in the SD-WAN member interface settings. The lowest possible cost is 0, which represents the most preferred link. In this example, DIA_1 and DIA_2 both have a cost of 0, while MPLS has a cost of 20 because it is used for backup.

6. In Interface preference, add the interfaces in order of preference when the cost of the links is tied. In this example, DIA_1, DIA_2, then MPLS.

   MPLS will always be chosen last, because it has the highest cost. DIA_1 and DIA_2 have the same cost, so an interface is selected based on their order in the Interface preference list.

7. Set Required SLA target to ensure that only links that pass your SLA target are chosen in this SD-WAN rule:

   1. Click in the Required SLA target field.

   2. In the Select Entries pane, click Create. The New Performace SLA pane opens.

   3. Set Name to BusinessCriticalApps_HC.

      This health check is used for business critical applications in your SD-WAN rule.

   4. Leave Protocol set to Ping, and add up to two servers, such as office.com and google.com.

   5. Set Participants to Specify, and add all three interfaces: DIA_1, DIA_2, and MPLS.

   6. Enable SLA Target.

      The attributes in your target determine the quality of your link. The SLA target of each link is compared when determining which link to use based on the lowest cost. Links that meet the SLA target are preferred over links that fail, and move to the next step of selection based on cost. If no links meet the SLA target, then they all move to the next step.

In this example, disable Latency threshold and Jitter threshold, and set Packet loss threshold to 1.

7. Click OK.

8. Select the new performance SLA to set it as the Required SLA target.

When multiple SLA targets are added, you can choose which target to use in the SD-WAN rule.

8. Click OK to create the SD-WAN rule.

To configure the SD-WAN rule and performance SLA checks for non-business critical application in the GUI:

1. Go to Network > SD-WAN, select the SD-WAN Rules tab, and click Create New.

2. Set the name to NonBusinessCriticalApps.

157

This rule will steer your non-business critical traffic to the appropriate link based on the Best Quality. No SLA target must be met, as the best link is selected based on the configured quality criteria and interface preference order.

3. Set Source address to all.

4. Under Destination, set Application to your required applications. In this example: Facebook, and Youtube.

5. Under Outgoing Interfaces, select Best Quality.

6. In Interface preference, add the interfaces in order of preference.

   By default, a more preferred link has an advantage of 10% over a less preferred link. For example, when latency is used, the preferred link's calculated latency = real latency / (1+10%).

The preferred link advantage can be customized in the CLI when the mode is priority (Best Quality) or auto:

```
config system sdwan
    config service
        edit <id>
            set link-cost-threshold <integer>
        next
    end
end
```

7. Create and apply a new performance SLA profile:

   1. Click in the Measured SLA field.

   2. In the drop-down list, click Create. The New Performace SLA pane opens.

   3. Set Name to NonBusinessCritical_HC.

      This health check is used for non-business critical applications in your SD-WAN rule.

   4. Leave Protocol set to Ping, and add up to two servers, such as youtube.com and facebook.com.

   5. Set Participants to Specify, and add the DIA_1 and DIA_2 interfaces. In this example, MPLS

158

is not used for non-business critical applications.

6. Leave SLA Target disabled.

7. Click OK.

8. Select the new performance SLA from the list to set it as the Measured SLA.

8. Set Quality criteria as required. In this example, Latency is selected.

For bandwidth related criteria, such as Downstream, Upstream, and Bandwidth (bi-directional), the selection is based on available bandwidth. An estimated bandwidth should be configured on the interface to provide a baseline, maximum available bandwidth.

9. Click OK to create the SD-WAN rule.

To configure the SD-WAN members, static route, and firewall policy in the CLI:

Configure the interfaces:

159

```
config system interface
    edit "port1"
        set ip <class_ip&net_netmask>
        set alias "DIA_1"
        set role wan
    next
    edit "port2"
        set ip <class_ip&net_netmask>
        set alias "DIA_2"
        set role wan
    next
    edit "port3"
        set ip <class_ip&net_netmask>
        set alias "MPLS"
        set role wan
    next
                        end
```

Configure the SD-WAN members:

```
config system sdwan
    set status enable
    config members
        edit 1
            set interface "port1"
            set gateway 172.16.20.2
        next
        edit 2
            set interface "port2"
            set gateway 172.17.80.2
        next
        edit 3
            set interface "port3"
```

```
            set gateway 10.100.20.2

            set cost 20

        next

    end

end
```

If no SD-WAN zone is specified, members are added to the
default virtual-wan-link zone.

3. Configure a static route.
4. Create a firewall policy to allow traffic out on SD-WAN, with
   an Application Control profile configured.

To configure the SD-WAN rule and performance SLA checks for business
critical application in the CLI:

Configure the BusinessCriticalApps_HC health-check:

```
config system sdwan
    config health-check
        edit "BusinessCriticalApps_HC"
            set server "office.com" "google.com"
            set members 1 2 3
            config sla
                edit 1
                    set link-cost-factor packet-loss
                    set packetloss-threshold 1
                next
            end
        next
    end
            end
```

Configure the BusinessCriticalApps service to use Lowest Cost (SLA):

```
config system sdwan
  config service
    edit 1
      set name "BusinessCriticalApps"
      set mode sla
      set src "all"
      set internet-service enable
      set internet-service-app-ctrl 17459 16541 33182 16177 34640
      config sla
        edit "BusinessCriticalApps_HC"
          set id 1
        next
      end
      set priority-members 1 2 3
    next
  end
        end
```

To configure the SD-WAN rule and performance SLA checks for non-business critical application in the CLI:

Configure the nonBusinessCriticalApps_HC health-check:

```
config system sdwan
  config health-check
    edit "NonBusinessCriticalApps_HC"
      set server "youtube.com" "facebook.com"
      set members 1 2
    next
  end
        end
```

Configure the NonBusinessCriticalApps service to use Lowest Cost (SLA):

```
config system sdwan
    config service
        edit 4
            set name "NonBusinessCriticalApps"
            set mode priority
            set src "all"
            set internet-service enable
            set internet-service-app-ctrl 15832 31077
            set health-check "NonBusinessCriticalApps_HC"
            set priority-members 1 2
        next
    end
            end
```

Verification

Check the following GUI pages, and run the following CLI commands to confirm that your traffic is being steered by the SD-WAN rules.

Health checks

To verify the status of each of the health checks in the GUI:

1. Go to Network > SD-WAN, select the Performance SLAs tab, and select each of the health checks from the list.

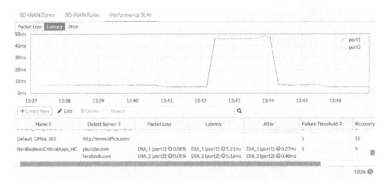

To verify the status of each of the health checks in the CLI:

diagnose sys sdwan health-check

Health Check(BusinessCritical_HC):

Seq(1 port1): state(alive), packet-loss(0.000%) latency(12.884), jitter(0.919) sla_map=0x1

Seq(2 port2): state(alive), packet-loss(0.000%) latency(13.018), jitter(0.723) sla_map=0x1

Seq(3 port3): state(alive), packet-loss(0.000%) latency(13.018), jitter(0.923) sla_map=0x1

Health Check(NonBusinessCritical_HC):

Seq(1 port1): state(alive), packet-loss(0.000%) latency(6.888), jitter(0.953) sla_map=0x0

Seq(2 port2): state(alive), packet-loss(0.000%) latency(6.805), jitter(0.830) sla_map=0x0

Rule members and hit count

To verify the active members and hit count of the SD-WAN rule in the GUI:

1. Go to Network > SD-WAN and select the SD-WAN Rules tab.

The interface that is currently selected by the rule has a checkmark next to its name in the Members column. Hover the cursor over the checkmark to open a tooltip that gives the reason why that member is selected. If multiple members are selected, only the highest ranked member is highlighted (unless the mode is Maximize Bandwidth (SLA)).

To verify the active members and hit count of the SD-WAN rule in the CLI:

diagnose sys sdwan service

Service(3): Address Mode(IPV4) flags=0x0

Gen(13), TOS(0x0/0x0), Protocol(0: 1->65535), Mode(sla), sla-compare-order

Members:

1: Seq_num(1 port1), alive, sla(0x1), cfg_order(0), cost(0), selected

2: Seq_num(2 port2), alive, sla(0x1), cfg_order(1), cost(0), selected

3: Seq_num(3 port3), alive, sla(0x1), cfg_order(2), cost(20), selected

Internet Service: Dropbox(4294836727,0,0,0 17459) Google.Docs(4294836992,0,0,0 16541) Microsoft.Office.365(4294837472,0,0,0 33182) Microsoft.Office.Online(4294837475,0,0,0 16177) SIP(4294837918,0,0,0 34640)

Src address:

0.0.0.0-255.255.255.255

Service(4): Address Mode(IPV4) flags=0x0

Gen(211), TOS(0x0/0x0), Protocol(0: 1->65535), Mode(priority), link-cost-factor(latency), link-cost-threshold(10), heath-check(NonBusinessCritical_HC)

Members:

1: Seq_num(1 port1), alive, latency: 5.712, selected

2: Seq_num(2 port2), alive, latency: 5.511, selected

Internet Service: Facebook(4294836806,0,0,0 15832) YouTube(4294838537,0,0,0 31077)

Src address:

0.0.0.0-255.255.255.255

Applications and sessions

To verify sessions in FortiView:

1. Go to a dashboard and add the FortiView Cloud Applications widget sorted by bytes.

2. Drill down on an application, such as YouTube, then select the Sessions tab.

To verify applications identified by Application Control in SD-WAN:

diagnose sys sdwan internet-service-app-ctrl-list

Steam(16518 4294838108): 23.6.148.10 6 443 Thu Apr 15 08:51:54 2021

Netflix(18155 4294837589): 54.160.93.182 6 443 Thu Apr 15 09:13:25 2021

Netflix(18155 4294837589): 54.237.226.164 6 443 Thu Apr 15 10:04:37 2021

Minecraft(27922 4294837491): 65.8.232.41 6 443 Thu Apr 15 09:12:19 2021

Minecraft(27922 4294837491): 65.8.232.46 6 443 Thu Apr 15 09:02:07 2021

Minecraft(27922 4294837491): 99.84.244.51 6 443 Thu Apr 15 10:23:57 2021

Minecraft(27922 4294837491): 99.84.244.63 6 443 Thu Apr 15 10:03:30 2021

YouTube(31077 4294838537): 74.125.69.93 6 443 Thu Apr 15 08:52:59 2021

YouTube(31077 4294838537): 108.177.112.136 6 443 Thu Apr 15 09:33:53 2021

YouTube(31077 4294838537): 142.250.1.93 6 443 Thu Apr 15 10:35:13 2021

...

DSCP tag-based traffic steering in SD-WAN

This document demonstrates the Differentiated Services Code Point (DSCP) tag-based traffic steering in Fortinet secure SD-WAN. You can use this guide as an example to deploy DSCP tag-based traffic steering in Fortinet secure SD-WAN.

DSCP tags are often used to categorize traffic to provide quality of service (QoS). Based on DSCP tags, you can provide SD-WAN traffic steering on an edge device.

In this example, we have two different departments at the Headquarters site - Customer Service and Marketing. Traffic from each of these departments is marked with separate DSCP tags by the core switch, and passes through the core switch to the edge FortiGate. The edge FortiGate reads the DSCP tags and steers traffic to the preferred interface based on the defined SD-WAN rules.

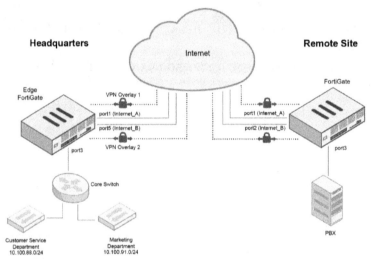

In our example, we consider two types of traffic - social media traffic and VoIP traffic. VoIP traffic from Customer Service is considered to be more important than social media traffic. Each of these traffic types is marked with a DSCP tag by the core switch - VoIP traffic is marked with the DSCP tag of 011100, and social media traffic is marked with the DSCP tag of 001100. The DSCP tagged traffic is then passed on to the edge FortiGate. The edge FortiGate identifies the DSCP tagged traffic and based on the defined SD-WAN rules, the edge FortiGate steers:

- VoIP traffic to the preferred VPN overlay with the least jitter in order to provide the best quality of voice communication with the remote VoIP server (PBX)

- Social media traffic to the preferred Internet link with a lower cost (less expensive and less reliable)

If you are familiar with SD-WAN configurations in FortiOS, you can directly jump to the Configuring SD-WAN rules section to learn how to configure the SD-WAN rules to perform traffic steering. Otherwise, you can proceed with all of the following topics to configure the edge FortiGate:

- Configuring IPsec tunnels
- Configuring SD-WAN zones
- Configuring firewall policies
- Configuring Performance SLA test
- Configuring SD-WAN rules
- Results

Configuring IPsec tunnels

In our example, we have two interfaces Internet_A (port1) and Internet_B(port5) on which we have configured IPsec tunnels Branch-HQ-A and Branch-HQ-B respectively. To learn how to configure IPsec tunnels, refer to the IPsec VPNs section.

After you have configured the IPsec tunnels, go to VPN > IPsec Tunnels to verify the IPsec tunnels.

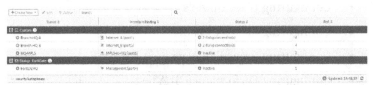

Configuring SD-WAN zones

In order for us to steer traffic based on SD-WAN rules, first we need to configure SD-WAN interface members and assign them to SD-WAN zones.

In our example, we created two SD-WAN zones. The virtual-wan-link SD-WAN zone for the underlay traffic passing through the Internet_A(port1) and Internet_B(port5) interfaces, and the Overlay SD-WAN zone for the overlay traffic passing through the Branch-HQ-A and Branch-HQ-B interfaces.

Go to Network > SD-WAN and select the SD-WAN Zones tab to verify the configurations.

In this screenshot, we have configured the Internet_A(port1) and Internet_B(port5) SD-WAN interface members with their Cost values being 0 and 10 respectively. A lower Cost value indicates that this member is the primary interface member, and is preferred more than a member with a higher Cost value when using the Lowest Cost (SLA) strategy.

We also need to configure a static route that points to the SD-WAN interface.

Configuring firewall policies

Configure firewall policies for both the overlay and underlay traffic.

In this example, the Overlay-out policy governs the overlay traffic and the SD-WAN-Out policy governs the underlay traffic. The firewall policies are configured accordingly.

Once created, verify the firewall policies by navigating to Policy & Objects > Firewall Policy:

The Security Profiles column indicates that the Overlay-out firewall policy for the overlay traffic is set up to not scan any traffic, while the SD-WAN-Out firewall policy is set to scan all web traffic to identify and govern social media traffic as Application Control profile is active.

Configuring Performance SLA test

Configure a performance SLA test that will be tied to the SD-WAN interface members we created and assigned to SD-WAN zones.

In this example, we created a Performance SLA test Default_DNS with Internet_A(port1) and Internet_B(port5) interface members as participants. We will use the created Performance SLA test to steer all web traffic passing through the underlays other than social media traffic based on the Lowest Cost (SLA) strategy.

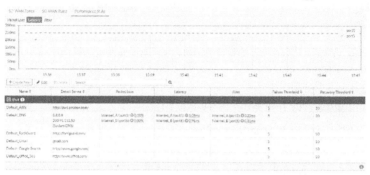

Configuring SD-WAN rules

Configure SD-WAN rules to govern the steering of DSCP tag-based traffic to the appropriate interfaces. Traffic will be steered based on the Criteria configured as part of the SD-WAN rules configuration.

In our example, we configured three different SD-WAN rules to govern DSCP tagged traffic. We have one SD-WAN rule each for VoIP traffic, social media traffic (Facebook in this case), and all other web traffic. VoIP traffic is always steered to either of the two overlay SD-WAN zones - VPN_A_tunnel(Branch-HQ-A) or VPN_B_tunnel(Branch-HQ-B). Similarly, social media traffic and other web traffic is always steered to either of the two underlay SD-WAN zones - Internet_A(port1) or Internet_B(port5). The interface that is preferred by the system over another depends upon the Criteria configured in the SD-WAN rule definition.

We configured the following SD-WAN rules:

- SD-WAN rule for VoIP traffic
- SD-WAN rule for social media traffic
- SD-WAN rule for other web traffic

SD-WAN rule for VoIP traffic

To configure SD-WAN rule for DSCP tagged VoIP traffic using the CLI:

```
config sys sdwan
    config service
        edit 5
            set name "VoIP-Steer"
            set mode priority
            set tos 0x70
            set tos-mask 0xf0
            set dst "all"
            set health-check "Default_DNS"
            set link-cost-factor jitter
            set priority-members 4 3
```

next

end

end

The VoIP-Steer SD-WAN rule configured above governs the DSCP tagged VoIP traffic.

DSCP values commonly are 6-bit binary numbers that are padded with zeros at the end. Therefore, in this example, VoIP traffic with DSCP tag 011100 will become 01110000. This 8-bit binary number 01110000 is represented in its hexadecimal form 0x70 as the tos (Type of Service bit pattern) value. The tos-mask (Type of Service evaluated bits) hexadecimal value of 0xf0 (binary 11110000) is used to check the four most significant bits from the tos value in this case. Hence, the first four bits of the tos (0111) will be used to match the first four bits of the DSCP tag in our policy above. Only the non-zero bit positions are used for comparison and the zero bit positions are ignored from the tos-mask.

We used the Best Quality strategy to define the Criteria to select the preferred interface from the overlay SD-WAN zone. With the Best Quality strategy selected, the interface with the best measured performance is selected. The system prefers the interface with the least Jitter.

SD-WAN rule for social media traffic

To configure SD-WAN rule for DSCP tagged social media traffic using the CLI:

FortiGate # config sys sdwan
    config service
        edit 3
            set name "Facebook-DSCP-steer"

```
        set tos 0x30
        set tos-mask 0xf0
        set dst "all"
        set priority-members 2 1
    end
```

The Facebook-DSCP-steer SD-WAN rule configured above governs the DSCP tagged social media traffic.

DSCP values commonly are 6-bit binary numbers that are padded with zeros at the end. Therefore, in this example, social media traffic with DSCP tag 001100 will become 00110000. This 8-bit binary number 00110000 is represented in its hexadecimal form 0x30 as the tos (Type of Service bit pattern) value. The tos-mask (Type of Service evaluated bits) hexadecimal value of 0xf0 (binary 11110000) is used to check the four most significant bits from the tos value in this case. Hence, the first four bits of the tos (0011) will be used to match the first four bits of the DSCP tag in our policy above. Only the non-zero bit positions are used for comparison and the zero bit positions are ignored from the tos-mask.

We used a manual strategy to select the preferred interface from the underlay SD-WAN zone. We manually select the preferred interface as Internet_B(port5) to steer all social media traffic to.

SD-WAN rule for other web traffic

To configure SD-WAN rule for all other web traffic using the CLI:

```
FortiGate # config sys sdwan
    config service
        edit 2
            set name "All-traffic"
            set mode sla
            set dst "all"
```

```
config sla
    edit "Default_DNS"
        set id 1
    next
end
set priority-members 1 2
end
```

The All-traffic SD-WAN rule configured above governs all other web traffic.

We used the Lowest Cost (SLA) strategy to define the Criteria to select the preferred interface from the underlay SD-WAN zone. With the Lowest Cost (SLA) strategy selected, the interface that meets the defined Performance SLA targets (Default_DNS in our case) is selected. When there is a tie, the interface with the lowest assigned Cost (Internet_A(port1) in our case) is selected.

Once configured, verify your SD-WAN rules by navigating to Network > SD-WAN and selecting the SD-WAN Rules tab.

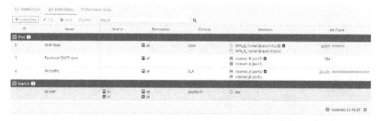

Results

The following sections show the function of the FortiGate and specifically of secure SD-WAN with respect to DSCP tagged traffic steering, and can be used to confirm that it is setup and running correctly:

- Verifying the DSCP tagged traffic on FortiGate

- Verifying service rules

- Verifying traffic steering as per the defined SD-WAN rules

- Verifying steered traffic leaving the required interface

Verifying the DSCP tagged traffic on FortiGate

To verify the incoming DSCP tagged traffic, we used packet sniffing and converting the sniffed traffic to a desired format.

For VoIP traffic that is marked with DSCP tag 0x70:

diagnose sniffer packet any '(ip and ip[1] & 0xfc == **0x70**)' 6 0 1

We used the open-source packet analyzer Wireshark to verify that VoIP traffic is tagged with the 0x70 DSCP tag.

For web traffic marked with DSCP tag 0x30:

diagnose sniffer packet any '(ip and ip[1] & 0xfc == **0x30**)' 6 0 1

We used the open-source packet analyzer Wireshark to verify that web traffic is tagged with the 0x30 DSCP tag.

Verifying service rules

The following CLI commands show the appropriate DSCP tags and the corresponding interfaces selected by the SD-WAN rules to steer traffic:

diagnose sys sdwan service

Service(5): Address Mode(IPV4) flags=0x0
   Gen(1), TOS(**0x70**/0xf0), Protocol(0: 1->65535), Mode(manual)
   Members:
      1: Seq_num(4 **Branch-HQ-B**), alive, selected
   Dst address:
      0.0.0.0-255.255.255.255

Service(3): Address Mode(IPV4) flags=0x0
   Gen(1), TOS(**0x30**/0xf0), Protocol(0: 1->65535), Mode(manual)
   Members:
      1: Seq_num(2 **port5**), alive, selected
   Dst address:
      0.0.0.0-255.255.255.255

Service(2): Address Mode(IPV4) flags=0x0

Gen(1), TOS(**0x0**/0x0), Protocol(0: 1->65535), Mode(sla), sla-compare-order

Members:

1: Seq_num(1 **port1**), alive, sla(0x1), cfg_order(0), cost(0), selected

2: Seq_num(2 **port5**), alive, sla(0x1), cfg_order(1), cost(10), selected

Dst address:

0.0.0.0-255.255.255.255

Verifying traffic steering as per the defined SD-WAN rules

Go to Network > SD-WAN and select the SD-WAN Rules tab to review the Hit Count on the appropriate SD-WAN interfaces.

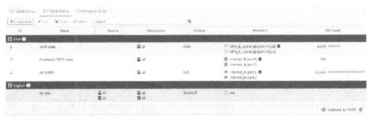

Verifying steered traffic leaving the required interface

Go to Dashboard > Top Policies to confirm that web traffic (port 443) flows through the right underlay interface members, and VoIP traffic flows through the right overlay interface member.

Web traffic leaves either Interface_A(port1) or Interface_B(port5):

VoIP traffic leaves the preferred VPN_B_Tunnel(Branch-HQ-B) interface:

ECMP support for the longest match in SD-WAN rule matching

The longest match SD-WAN rule can match ECMP best routes. The rule will select the egress ports on ECMP specific routes, and not the less specific routes, to transport traffic.

The service mode determines which egress port on the ECMP specific routes is selected to forward traffic:

- Manual (manual): The first configured alive port is selected.

- Best Quality (priority): The best quality port is selected.

- Lowest Cost (sla): The first configured or lower cost port in SLA is selected.

Example

By default, SD-WAN selects the outgoing interface from all of the links that have valid routes to the destination. In some cases, it is required that only the links that have the best (or longest match) routes (single or ECMP) to the destination are considered.

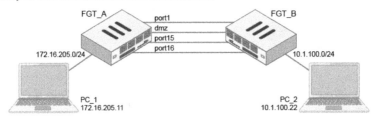

In this example, four SD-WAN members in two zones are configured. The remote PC (PC_2 - 10.1.100.22) is accessible on port15 and port16, even though there are valid routes for all of the SD-WAN members. A single SD-WAN service rule is configured that allows traffic to balanced between all four of the members, but only chooses between port15 and port16 for the specific 10.1.100.22 address.

A performance SLA health check is configured to monitor 10.1.100.2. An SD-WAN service rule in Lowest Cost (SLA) mode is configured to select the best interface to steer the traffic. In the rule, the method of selecting a member if more than one meets the SLA (tie-break) is configured to select members that meet the SLA and match the longest prefix in the routing table (fib-best-match). If there are multiple ECMP routes with the same destination, the FortiGate will take the longest (or best) match in the routing table, and choose from those interface members.

To configure the SD-WAN:

```
config system sdwan
    config zone
        edit "virtual-wan-link"
        next
        edit "z1"
        next
    end
    config members
        edit 1
            set interface "port1"
            set gateway 172.16.200.2
        next
        edit 2
            set interface "dmz"
            set gateway 172.16.208.2
        next
        edit 3
            set interface "port15"
            set zone "z1"
            set gateway 172.16.209.2
        next
        edit 4
            set interface "port16"
            set zone "z1"
            set gateway 172.16.210.2
        next
    end
    config health-check
        edit "1"
            set server "10.1.100.2"
            set members 0
```

```
config sla
    edit 1
    next
    end
next
end
config service
    edit 1
        set name "1"
        set mode sla
        set dst "all"
        set src "172.16.205.0"
        config sla
            edit "1"
                set id 1
            next
        end
        set priority-members 1 2 3 4
        set tie-break fib-best-match
    next
    end
end
```

To check the results:

The debug shows the SD-WAN service rule. All of the members meet SLA, and because no specific costs are attached to the members, the egress interface is selected based on the interface priority order that is configured in the rule:

FGT_A (root) # diagnose sys sdwan service

Service(1): Address Mode(IPV4) flags=0x200 use-shortcut-sla

Gen(4), TOS(0x0/0x0), Protocol(0: 1->65535), Mode(sla), sla-compare-order

Members(4):

1: Seq_num(1 port1), alive, sla(0x1), gid(0), cfg_order(0), cost(0), selected

2: Seq_num(2 dmz), alive, sla(0x1), gid(0), cfg_order(1), cost(0), selected

3: Seq_num(3 port15), alive, sla(0x1), gid(0), cfg_order(2), cost(0), selected

4: Seq_num(4 port16), alive, sla(0x1), gid(0), cfg_order(3), cost(0), selected

Src address(1):

172.16.205.0-172.16.205.255

Dst address(1):

0.0.0.0-255.255.255.255

The routing table shows that there are ECMP default routes on all of the members, and ECMP specific (or best) routes only on port15 and port16:

FGT_A (root) # get router info routing-table static

Routing table for VRF=0

S*   0.0.0.0/0 [1/0] via 172.16.200.2, port1

          [1/0] via 172.16.208.2, dmz

          [1/0] via 172.16.209.2, port15

          [1/0] via 172.16.210.2, port16

S   10.1.100.22/32 [10/0] via 172.16.209.2, port15

          [10/0] via 172.16.210.2, port16

Because tie-break is set to fib-best-match, the first configured member from port15 and port16 is selected to forward traffic to PC_2. For all other traffic, the first configured member from all four of the interfaces is selected to forward traffic.

On PC-1, generate traffic to PC-2:

ping 10.1.100.22

On FGT_A, sniff for traffic sent to PC_2:

diagnose sniffer packet any 'host 10.1.100.22' 4

interfaces=[any]

filters=[host 10.1.100.22]

2.831299 port5 in 172.16.205.11 -> 10.1.100.22: icmp: echo request

> 2.831400 port15 out 172.16.205.11 -> 10.1.100.22: icmp: echo request

> Traffic is leaving on port15, the first configured member from port15 and port16.

Override quality comparisons in SD-WAN longest match rule matching

In SD-WAN rules, the longest match routes will override the quality comparisons when all of the specific routes are out of SLA.

With this feature in an SD-WAN rule:

- Lowest Cost (sla): Even though all of the egress ports on specific routes (longest matched routes) are out of SLA, the SD-WAN rule still selects the first configured or lower-cost port from the egress ports to forward traffic.

- Best Quality (priority): Even though the egress ports on specific routes (longest matched routes) have worse quality that all other ports on less specific routes, the SD-WAN rule still selects the best quality port from the ports on specific routes to forward traffic.

This features avoids a situation where, if the members on specific routes (longest matched routes) are out of SLA or have worse quality, the traffic might be forwarded to the wrong members in SLA (higher quality) on the default or aggregate routes.

Example

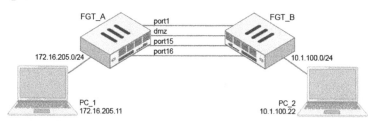

In this example, four SD-WAN members in two zones are configured. The remote PC (PC_2 - 10.1.100.22) is accessible on port15 and port16, even though there are valid routes for all of the SD-WAN members. A single SD-WAN service rule is configured that allows traffic to balanced between all four of the members, but only chooses between port15 and port16 for the specific 10.1.100.22 address. If neither port15 nor port16 meet the SLAs, traffic will be forwarded on one of these interfaces, instead of on port1 or dmz.

A performance SLA health check is configured to monitor 10.1.100.2. An SD-WAN service rule in Lowest Cost (SLA) mode is configured to select the best interface to steer the traffic. In the rule, the method of selecting a member if more than one meets the SLA (tie-break) is configured to select members that meet the SLA and match the longest prefix in the routing table (fib-best-match). If there are multiple ECMP routes with the same destination, the FortiGate will take the longest (or best) match in the routing table, and choose from those interface members.

To configure the SD-WAN:

```
config system sdwan
  config zone
    edit "virtual-wan-link"
    next
    edit "z1"
    next
  end
  config members
    edit 1
      set interface "port1"
      set gateway 172.16.200.2
    next
    edit 2
      set interface "dmz"
      set gateway 172.16.208.2
    next
    edit 3
      set interface "port15"
      set zone "z1"
      set gateway 172.16.209.2
    next
    edit 4
      set interface "port16"
      set zone "z1"
      set gateway 172.16.210.2
    next
```

```
        end
    config health-check
        edit "1"
            set server "10.1.100.2"
            set members 0
            config sla
                edit 1
                next
            end
        next
    end
    config service
        edit 1
            set name "1"
            set mode sla
            set dst "all"
            set src "172.16.205.0"
            config sla
                edit "1"
                    set id 1
                next
            end
            set priority-members 1 2 3 4
            set tie-break fib-best-match
        next
    end
end
```

To check the results:

The debug shows the SD-WAN service rule. Both port15 and port16 are up, but out of SLA:

FGT_A (root) # diagnose sys sdwan service

Service(1): Address Mode(IPV4) flags=0x200 use-shortcut-sla

Gen(3), TOS(0x0/0x0), Protocol(0: 1->65535), Mode(sla), sla-compare-order

Members(4):

1: Seq_num(1 port1), alive, sla(0x1), gid(0), cfg_order(0), cost(0), selected

2: Seq_num(2 dmz), alive, sla(0x1), gid(0), cfg_order(1), cost(0), selected

3: Seq_num(3 port15), alive, **sla(0x0)**, gid(0), cfg_order(2), cost(0), selected

4: Seq_num(4 port16), alive, **sla(0x0)**, gid(0), cfg_order(3), cost(0), selected

Src address(1):

172.16.205.0-172.16.205.255

Dst address(1):

0.0.0.0-255.255.255.255

The routing table shows that there are ECMP default routes on all of the members, and ECMP specific (or best) routes only on port15 and port16:

FGT_A (root) # get router info routing-table static

Routing table for VRF=0

S*   0.0.0.0/0 [1/0] via 172.16.200.2, port1

          [1/0] via 172.16.208.2, dmz

          [1/0] via 172.16.209.2, port15

          [1/0] via 172.16.210.2, port16

S   10.1.100.22/32 [10/0] via 172.16.209.2, port15

          [10/0] via 172.16.210.2, port16

Because tie-break is set to fib-best-match, even though both port15 and port16 are out of SLA, the first configured member of the two (port15) is selected to forward traffic to PC_2. For all other traffic, the first configured member from all of the interfaces that are in SLA is selected to forward traffic (port1).

On PC-1, generate traffic to PC-2:

> ping 10.1.100.22

On FGT_A, sniff for traffic sent to PC_2:

diagnose sniffer packet any 'host 10.1.100.22' 4

interfaces=[any]

filters=[host 10.1.100.22]

2.831299 port5 in 172.16.205.11 -> 10.1.100.22: icmp: echo request

> 2.831400 port15 out 172.16.205.11 -> 10.1.100.22: icmp: echo request

Traffic is leaving on port15, the first configured member from port15 and port16, even though both are out of SLA.

Use an application category as an SD-WAN rule destination

An application category can be selected as an SD-WAN service rule destination criterion. Previously, only application groups or individual applications could be selected.

config system sdwan

  config service

    edit <id>

      set internet-service enable

      set internet-service-app-ctrl-category <id_1> <id_2> ... <id_n>

    next

  end

end

To view the detected application categories details based on category ID, use diagnose sys sdwan internet-service-app-ctrl-category-list <id>.

Example

In this example, traffic steering is applied to traffic detected as video/audio (category ID 5) or email (category ID 21) and applies the lowest cost (SLA) strategy to this traffic. When costs are tied, the priority goes to member 1, dmz.

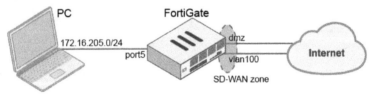

To configure application categories as an SD-WAN rule destination:

  Configure the SD-WAN settings:

  config system sdwan

    set status enable

    config zone

      edit "virtual-wan-link"

```
        next
    end
    config members
        edit 1
            set interface "dmz"
            set gateway 172.16.208.2
        next
        edit 2
            set interface "vlan100"
            set gateway 172.16.206.2
        next
    end
    config health-check
        edit "1"
            set server "8.8.8.8"
            set protocol dns
            set members 0
            config sla
                edit 1
                next
            end
        next
    end
            end
```

Configure the SD-WAN rule to use application categories 5 and 21:

```
config system sdwan
    config service
        edit 1
            set name "1"
            set mode sla
            set src "172.16.205.0"
```

```
        set internet-service enable
        set internet-service-app-ctrl-category 5 21
        config sla
            edit "1"
                set id 1
            next
        end
        set priority-members 1 2
    next
  end
                end
```

Configure the firewall policy:

```
config firewall policy
    edit 1
        set srcintf "port5"
        set dstintf "virtual-wan-link"
        set action accept
        set srcaddr 172.16.205.0
        set dstaddr "all"
        set schedule "always"
        set service "ALL"
        set utm-status enable
        set ssl-ssh-profile "certificate-inspection"
        set application-list "g-default"
    next
                end
```

Verify that the traffic is sent over dmz:

```
# diagnose firewall proute list
list route policy info(vf=root):

id=2133590017(0x7f2c0001)  vwl_service=1(1)  vwl_mbr_seq=1  2
dscp_tag=0xff 0xff flags=0x0 tos=0x00 tos_mask=0x00 protocol=0
```

sport=0-65535 uf=0 dport=1-65535 **path(2)** **oif=5(dmz)**
oif=95(vlan100)

source(1): 172.16.205.0-172.16.205.255

destination wildcard(1): 0.0.0.0/0.0.0.0

internet service(2): (null)(0,5,0,0,0) (null)(0,21,0,0,0)

hit_count=469 last_used=2021-12-15 15:06:05

View some videos and emails on the PC, then verify the detected application details for each category:

diagnose sys sdwan internet-service-app-ctrl-category-list 5

YouTube(31077 4294838537): 142.250.217.110 6 443 Wed Dec 15 15:39:50 2021

YouTube(31077 4294838537): 173.194.152.89 6 443 Wed Dec 15 15:37:20 2021

YouTube(31077 4294838537): 173.194.152.170 6 443 Wed Dec 15 15:37:37 2021

YouTube(31077 4294838537): 209.52.146.205 6 443 Wed Dec 15 15:37:19 2021

diagnose sys sdwan internet-service-app-ctrl-category-list 21

Gmail(15817 4294836957): **172.217.14.197** 6 443 Wed Dec 15 15:39:47 2021

Verify that the captured email traffic is sent over dmz:

diagnose sniffer packet any 'host 172.217.14.197' 4

interfaces=[any]

filters=[host 172.217.14.197]

5.079814 **dmz** out 172.16.205.100.60592 -> 172.217.14.197.443: psh 2961561240 ack 2277134591

Edit the SD-WAN rule so that dmz has a higher cost and vlan100 is preferred.

Verify that the traffic is now sent over vlan100:

diagnose firewall proute list

list route policy info(vf=root):

id=2134048769(0x7f330001) vwl_service=1(1) vwl_mbr_seq=2 1 dscp_tag=0xff 0xff flags=0x0 tos=0x00 tos_mask=0x00 protocol=0 sport=0-65535   nf=0   dport=1-65535 **path(2)   oif=95(vlan100) oif=5(dmz)**

source(1): 172.16.205.0-172.16.205.255

destination wildcard(1): 0.0.0.0/0.0.0.0

internet service(2): (null)(0,5,0,0,0) (null)(0,21,0,0,0)

> hit_count=635 last_used=2021-12-15 15:55:43
>
> # diagnose sniffer packet any 'host 172.217.14.197' 4
>
> interfaces=[any]
>
> filters=[host 172.217.14.197]
>
> 304.625168 **vlan100** in 172.16.205.100.60592 -> 172.217.14.197.443: psh 2961572711 ack 2277139565

Troubleshooting SD-WAN

The following topics provide instructions on SD-WAN troubleshooting:

- Tracking SD-WAN sessions
- Understanding SD-WAN related logs
- SD-WAN related diagnose commands
- SD-WAN bandwidth monitoring service
- Using SNMP to monitor health check

Tracking SD-WAN sessions

You can check the destination interface in Dashboard > FortiView Sessions in order to see which port the traffic is being forwarded to.

The example below demonstrates a source-based load-balance between two SD-WAN members:

- If the source IP address is an even number, it will go to port13.

- If the source IP address is an odd number, it will go to port12.

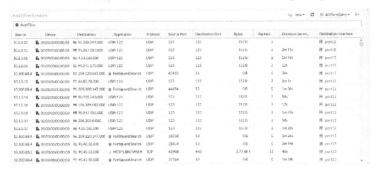

Understanding SD-WAN related logs

This topic lists the SD-WAN related logs and explains when the logs will be triggered.

Health-check detects a failure:

- When health-check detects a failure, it will record a log:

  1:             date=2021-04-20   time=17:06:31
  eventtime=1618963591590008160   tz="-0700"
  logid="0100022921"   type="event"   subtype="system"
  level="critical" vd="root" logdesc="Routing information
  changed" name="test" interface="R150" status="down"
  msg="Static route on interface R150 may be removed by
  health-check test. Route: (10.100.1.2->10.100.2.22 ping-
  down)"

- When health-check detects a recovery, it will record a log:

  2:             date=2021-04-20   time=17:11:46
  eventtime=1618963906950174240   tz="-0700"
  logid="0100022921"   type="event"   subtype="system"
  level="critical" vd="root" logdesc="Routing information
  changed" name="test" interface="R150" status="up"
  msg="Static route on interface R150 may be added by health-
  check test. Route: (10.100.1.2->10.100.2.22 ping-up)"

Health-check has an SLA target and detects SLA qualification changes:

- When health-check has an SLA target and detects
  SLA changes, and changes to fail:

  1:             date=2021-04-20   time=21:32:33
  eventtime=1618979553388763760   tz="-0700"
  logid="0113022923"   type="event"   subtype="sdwan"
  level="notice"   vd="root"   logdesc="SDWAN   status"
  eventtype="Health Check" healthcheck="test" slatargetid=1
  oldvalue="2" newvalue="1" msg="Number of pass member
  changed."

  2:             date=2021-04-20   time=21:32:33
  eventtime=1618979553388751880   tz="-0700"
  logid="0113022923"   type="event"   subtype="sdwan"
  level="notice"   vd="root"   logdesc="SDWAN   status"
  eventtype="Health Check" healthcheck="test" slatargetid=1
  member="1" msg="Member status changed. Member out-of-
  sla."

- When health-check has an SLA target and detects SLA changes, and changes to pass:

  ```
  1:              date=2021-04-20              time=21:38:49
  eventtime=1618979929908765200              tz="-0700"
  logid="0113022923"      type="event"      subtype="sdwan"
  level="notice"    vd="root"    logdesc="SDWAN    status"
  eventtype="Health Check" healthcheck="test" slatargetid=1
  oldvalue="1" newvalue="2" msg="Number of pass member
  changed."
  ```

  ```
  2:              date=2021-04-20              time=21:38:49
  eventtime=1618979929908754060              tz="-0700"
  logid="0113022923"      type="event"      subtype="sdwan"
  level="information"  vd="root"  logdesc="SDWAN  status"
  eventtype="Health Check" healthcheck="test" slatargetid=1
  member="1" msg="Member status changed. Member in sla."
  ```

SD-WAN calculates a link's session/bandwidth over/under its ratio and stops/resumes traffic:

- When SD-WAN calculates a link's session/bandwidth over its configured ratio and stops forwarding traffic:

  ```
  1:              date=2021-04-20              time=21:55:14
  eventtime=1618980914728863220              tz="-0700"
  logid="0113022924"      type="event"      subtype="sdwan"
  level="notice" vd="root" logdesc="SDWAN volume status"
  eventtype="Volume"    interface="R160"    member="2"
  msg="Member enters into conservative status with limited
  ablity to receive new sessions for too much traffic."
  ```

- When SD-WAN calculates a link's session/bandwidth according to its ratio and resumes forwarding traffic:

  ```
  2:              date=2021-04-20              time=22:12:52
  eventtime=1618981972698753360              tz="-0700"
  logid="0113022924"      type="event"      subtype="sdwan"
  level="notice" vd="root" logdesc="SDWAN volume status"
  eventtype="Volume"    interface="R160"    member="2"
  msg="Member resume normal status to receive new sessions
  for internal adjustment"
  ```

The SLA mode service rule's SLA qualified member changes:

- When the SLA mode service rule's SLA qualified member changes. In this example R150 fails the SLA check, but is still alive:

```
1:          date=2021-04-20                    time=22:40:46
eventtime=1618983646428803040                  tz="-0700"
logid="0113022923"    type="event"    subtype="sdwan"
level="notice"   vd="root"   logdesc="SDWAN     status"
eventtype="Service" serviceid=1 service="test" seq="2,1"
msg="Service prioritized by SLA will be redirected in
sequence order."
```

- When the SLA mode service rule's SLA qualified member changes. In this example R150 changes from fail to pass:

```
2:          date=2021-04-20                    time=22:41:51
eventtime=1618983711678827920                  tz="-0700"
logid="0113022923"    type="event"    subtype="sdwan"
level="notice"   vd="root"   logdesc="SDWAN     status"
eventtype="Service" serviceid=1 service="test" seq="1,2"
msg="Service prioritized by SLA will be redirected in
sequence order."
```

The priority mode service rule member's link status changes:

- When priority mode service rule member's link status changes. In this example R150 changes to better than R160, and both are still alive:

```
1:          date=2021-04-20                    time=22:56:55
eventtime=1618984615708804760                  tz="-0700"
logid="0113022923"    type="event"    subtype="sdwan"
level="notice"   vd="root"   logdesc="SDWAN     status"
eventtype="Service"         serviceid=1        service="test"
metric="packet-loss" seq="2,1" msg="Service prioritized by
performance metric will be redirected in sequence order."
```

- When priority mode service rule member's link status changes. In this example R160 changes to better than R150, and both are still alive:

```
2:          date=2021-04-20                    time=22:56:58
eventtime=1618984618278852140                  tz="-0700"
logid="0113022923"    type="event"    subtype="sdwan"
level="notice"   vd="root"   logdesc="SDWAN     status"
eventtype="Service"         serviceid=1        service="test"
metric="packet-loss" seq="1,2" msg="Service prioritized by
performance metric will be redirected in sequence order."
```

SD-WAN member is used in service and it fails the health-check:

- When SD-WAN member fails the health-check, it will stop forwarding traffic:

1:        date=2021-04-20   time=23:04:32 eventtime=1618985072898756700   tz="-0700" logid="0113022923"   type="event"   subtype="sdwan" level="notice"   vd="root"   logdesc="SDWAN   status" eventtype="Service"   interface="R150"   member="1" serviceid=1 service="test" gateway=10.100.1.1 msg="Member link is unreachable or miss threshold. Stop forwarding traffic. "

- When SD-WAN member passes the health-check again, it will resume forwarding logs:

2:        date=2021-04-20   time=23:06:08 eventtime=1618985168018789600   tz="-0700" logid="0113022923"   type="event"   subtype="sdwan" level="notice"   vd="root"   logdesc="SDWAN   status" eventtype="Service"   interface="R150"   member="1" serviceid=1 service="test" gateway=10.100.1.1 msg="Member link is available. Start forwarding traffic. "

Load-balance mode service rule's SLA qualified member changes:

- When load-balance mode service rule's SLA qualified member changes. In this example R150 changes to not meet SLA:

1:        date=2021-04-20   time=23:10:24 eventtime=1618985425048820800   tz="-0700" logid="0113022923"   type="event"   subtype="sdwan" level="notice"   vd="root"   logdesc="SDWAN   status" eventtype="Service"   serviceid=1   service="test" member="2(R160)" msg="Service will be load balanced among members with available routing."

- When load-balance mode service rule's SLA qualified member changes. In this example R150 changes to meet SLA:

2:        date=2021-04-20   time=23:11:34 eventtime=1618985494478807100   tz="-0700" logid="0113022923"   type="event"   subtype="sdwan" level="notice"   vd="root"   logdesc="SDWAN   status" eventtype="Service"   serviceid=1   service="test" member="2(R160),1(R150)" msg="Service will be load balanced among members with available routing."

SLA link status logs, generated with interval sla-fail-log-period or sla-pass-log-period:

- When SLA fails, SLA link status logs will be generated with interval sla-fail-log-period:

1:          date=2021-04-20   time=23:18:10
eventtime=1618985890469018260   tz="-0700"
logid="0113022925"   type="event"   subtype="sdwan"
level="notice" vd="root" logdesc="SDWAN SLA information"
eventtype="SLA"   healthcheck="test"   slatargetid=1
interface="R150" status="up" latency="0.061" jitter="0.004"
packetloss="2.000%"   inbandwidthavailable="0kbps"
outbandwidthavailable="200.00Mbps"
bibandwidthavailable="200.00Mbps"
inbandwidthused="1kbps"   outbandwidthused="1kbps"
bibandwidthused="2kbps"   slamap="0x0"
metric="packetloss" msg="Health Check SLA status. SLA
failed due to being over the performance metric threshold."

- When SLA passes, SLA link status logs will be generated with
  interval sla-pass-log-period:

2:          date=2021-04-20   time=23:18:12
eventtime=1618985892509027220   tz="-0700"
logid="0113022925"   type="event"   subtype="sdwan"
level="information"   vd="root"   logdesc="SDWAN   SLA
information"   eventtype="SLA"   healthcheck="test"
slatargetid=1 interface="R150" status="up" latency="0.060"
jitter="0.003"   packetloss="0.000%"
inbandwidthavailable="0kbps"
outbandwidthavailable="200.00Mbps"
bibandwidthavailable="200.00Mbps"
inbandwidthused="1kbps"   outbandwidthused="1kbps"
bibandwidthused="2kbps" slamap="0x1" msg="Health Check
SLA status."

SD-WAN related diagnose commands

This topic lists the SD-WAN related diagnose commands and related output.

To check SD-WAN health-check status:

FGT # diagnose sys sdwan health-check

Health Check(server):

Seq(1 R150): state(alive), packet-loss(0.000%) latency(0.110), jitter(0.024) sla_map=0x0

Seq(2 R160): state(alive), packet-loss(0.000%) latency(0.068), jitter(0.009) sla_map=0x0

FGT # diagnose sys sdwan health-check

Health Check(ping):

Seq(1 R150): state(alive), packet-loss(0.000%) latency(0.100), jitter(0.017) sla_map=0x0

Seq(2 R160): state(dead), packet-loss(100.000%) sla_map=0x0

FGT # diagnose sys sdwan health-check google

Health Check(google):

Seq(1 R150): state(alive), packet-loss(0.000%) latency(0.081), jitter(0.019) sla_map=0x0

Seq(2 R160): state(alive), packet-loss(0.000%) latency(0.060), jitter(0.004) sla_map=0x0

To check SD-WAN member status:

- When SD-WAN load-balance mode is source-ip-based/source-dest-ip-based.

FGT # diagnose sys sdwan member

Member(1): interface: R150, gateway: 10.100.1.1 2000:10:100:1::1, priority: 0 1024, weight: 0

Member(2): interface: R160, gateway: 10.100.1.5 2000:10:100:1::5, priority: 0 1024, weight: 0

- When SD-WAN load-balance mode is weight-based.

FGT # diagnose sys sdwan member

Member(1): interface: R150, gateway: 10.100.1.1 2000:10:100:1::1, priority: 0 1024, weight: 33

Session count: 15

Member(2): interface: R160, gateway: 10.100.1.5 2000:10:100:1::5, priority: 0 1024, weight: 66

Session count: 1

When SD-WAN load-balance mode is measured-volume-based.

Both members are under volume and still have room:

FGT # diagnose sys sdwan member

Member(1): interface: R150, gateway: 10.100.1.1 2000:10:100:1::1, priority: 0 1024, weight: 33

Config volume ratio: 33, last reading: 218067B, volume room 33MB

Member(2): interface: R160, gateway: 10.100.1.5 2000:10:100:1::5, priority: 0 1024, weight: 66

Config volume ratio: 66, last reading: 202317B, volume room 66MB

Some members are overloaded and some still have room:

FGT # diagnose sys sdwan member

Member(1): interface: R150, gateway: 10.100.1.1 2000:10:100:1::1, priority: 0 1024, weight: 0

Config volume ratio: 33, last reading: 1287767633B, overload volume 517MB

Member(2): interface: R160, gateway: 10.100.1.5 2000:10:100:1::5, priority: 0 1024, weight: 63

Config volume ratio: 66, last reading: 1686997898B, volume room 63MB

When SD-WAN load balance mode is usage-based/spillover.

When no spillover occurs:

FGT # diagnose sys sdwan member

Member(1): interface: R150, gateway: 10.100.1.1 2000:10:100:1::1, priority: 0 1024, weight: 255

  Egress-spillover-threshold: 400kbit/s, ingress-spillover-threshold: 300kbit/s

  Egress-overbps=0, ingress-overbps=0

Member(2): interface: R160, gateway: 10.100.1.5 2000:10:100:1::5, priority: 0 1024, weight: 254

  Egress-spillover-threshold: 0kbit/s, ingress-spillover-threshold: 0kbit/s

  Egress-overbps=0, ingress-overbps=0

When member has reached limit and spillover occurs:

FGT # diagnose sys sdwan member

Member(1): interface: R150, gateway: 10.100.1.1 2000:10:100:1::1, priority: 0 1024, weight: 255

  Egress-spillover-threshold: 400kbit/s, ingress-spillover-threshold: 300kbit/s

  Egress-overbps=1, ingress-overbps=0

Member(2): interface: R160, gateway: 10.100.1.5 2000:10:100:1::5, priority: 0 1024, weight: 254

  Egress-spillover-threshold: 0kbit/s, ingress-spillover-threshold: 0kbit/s

  Egress-overbps=0, ingress-overbps=0

You can also use the diagnose netlink dstmac list command to check if you are over the limit.

FGT # diagnose netlink dstmac list R150

dev=R150 mac=00:00:00:00:00:00 vwl rx_tcp_mss=0 tx_tcp_mss=0   egress_overspill_threshold=50000 egress_bytes=100982   egress_over_bps=1

ingress_overspill_threshold=37500   ingress_bytes=40
ingress_over_bps=0   sampler_rate=0   vwl_zone_id=1
intf_qua=0

To check SD-WAN service rules status:

Manual mode service rules.

FGT # diagnose sys sdwan service

Service(1): Address Mode(IPV4) flags=0x200

  Gen(1), TOS(0x0/0x0), Protocol(0: 1->65535), Mode(manual)

  Members(2):

    1: Seq_num(1 R150), alive, selected

    2: Seq_num(2 R160), alive, selected

  Dst address(1):

    10.100.21.0-10.100.21.255

Auto mode service rules.

FGT # diagnose sys sdwan service

Service(1): Address Mode(IPV4) flags=0x200

  Gen(1), TOS(0x0/0x0), Protocol(0: 1->65535), Mode(auto), link-cost-factor(latency), link-cost-threshold(10), heath-check(ping)

  Members(2):

    1: Seq_num(2 R160), alive, latency: 0.066, selected

    2: Seq_num(1 R150), alive, latency: 0.093

  Dst address(1):

    10.100.21.0-10.100.21.255

Priority mode service rules.

FGT # diagnose sys sdwan service

Service(1): Address Mode(IPV4) flags=0x200

  Gen(1), TOS(0x0/0x0), Protocol(0: 1->65535), Mode(priority), link-cost-factor(latency), link-cost-threshold(10), heath-check(ping)

Members(2):

    1: Seq_num(2 R160), alive, latency: 0.059, selected

    2: Seq_num(1 R150), alive, latency: 0.077, selected

Dst address(1):

    10.100.21.0-10.100.21.255

Load-balance mode service rules.

FGT # diagnose sys sdwan service

Service(1): Address Mode(IPV4) flags=0x200

  Gen(1), TOS(0x0/0x0), Protocol(0: 1->65535), Mode(load-balance hash-mode=round-robin)

  Members(2):

    1: Seq_num(1 R150), alive, sla(0x1), gid(2), num of pass(1), selected

    2: Seq_num(2 R160), alive, sla(0x1), gid(2), num of pass(1), selected

  Dst address(1):

    10.100.21.0-10.100.21.255

SLA mode service rules.

FGT # diagnose sys sdwan service

Service(1): Address Mode(IPV4) flags=0x200

  Gen(1), TOS(0x0/0x0), Protocol(0: 1->65535), Mode(sla), sla-compare-order

  Members(2):

    1: Seq_num(1 R150), alive, sla(0x1), gid(0), cfg_order(0), cost(0), selected

    2: Seq_num(2 R160), alive, sla(0x1), gid(0), cfg_order(1), cost(0), selected

  Dst address(1):

    10.100.21.0-10.100.21.255

To check interface logs from the past 15 minutes:

FGT (root) # diagnose sys sdwan intf-sla-log R150

Timestamp: Wed Apr 21 16:58:27 2021, used inbandwidth: 655bps, used outbandwidth: 81655306bps, used bibandwidth: 81655961bps, tx bys: 3413479982bytes, rx bytes: 207769bytes.

Timestamp: Wed Apr 21 16:58:37 2021, used inbandwidth: 649bps, used outbandwidth: 81655540bps, used bibandwidth: 81656189bps, tx bys: 3515590414bytes, rx bytes: 208529bytes.

Timestamp: Wed Apr 21 16:58:47 2021, used inbandwidth: 655bps, used outbandwidth: 81655546bps, used bibandwidth: 81656201bps, tx bys: 3617700886bytes, rx bytes: 209329bytes.

Timestamp: Wed Apr 21 16:58:57 2021, used inbandwidth: 620bps, used outbandwidth: 81671580bps, used bibandwidth: 81672200bps, tx bys: 3719811318bytes, rx bytes: 210089bytes.

Timestamp: Wed Apr 21 16:59:07 2021, used inbandwidth: 620bps, used outbandwidth: 81671580bps, used bibandwidth: 81672200bps, tx bys: 3821921790bytes, rx bytes: 210889bytes.

Timestamp: Wed Apr 21 16:59:17 2021, used inbandwidth: 665bps, used outbandwidth: 81688152bps, used bibandwidth: 81688817bps, tx bys: 3924030936bytes, rx bytes: 211926bytes.

Timestamp: Wed Apr 21 16:59:27 2021, used inbandwidth: 671bps, used outbandwidth: 81688159bps, used bibandwidth: 81688830bps, tx bys: 4026141408bytes, rx bytes: 212726bytes.

To check SLA logs in the past 10 minutes:

FGT (root) # diagnose sys sdwan sla-log ping 1

Timestamp: Wed Apr 21 17:10:11 2021, vdom root, health-check ping, interface: R150, status: up, latency: 0.079, jitter: 0.023, packet loss: 0.000%.

Timestamp: Wed Apr 21 17:10:12 2021, vdom root, health-check ping, interface: R150, status: up, latency: 0.079, jitter: 0.023, packet loss: 0.000%.

Timestamp: Wed Apr 21 17:10:12 2021, vdom root, health-check ping, interface: R150, status: up, latency: 0.081, jitter: 0.024, packet loss: 0.000%.

Timestamp: Wed Apr 21 17:10:13 2021, vdom root, health-check ping, interface: R150, status: up, latency: 0.081, jitter: 0.025, packet loss: 0.000%.

Timestamp: Wed Apr 21 17:10:13 2021, vdom root, health-check ping, interface: R150, status: up, latency: 0.082, jitter: 0.026, packet loss: 0.000%.

Timestamp: Wed Apr 21 17:10:14 2021, vdom root, health-check ping, interface: R150, status: up, latency: 0.083, jitter: 0.026, packet loss: 0.000%.

Timestamp: Wed Apr 21 17:10:14 2021, vdom root, health-check ping, interface: R150, status: up, latency: 0.084, jitter: 0.026, packet loss: 0.000%.

To check Application Control used in SD-WAN and the matching IP addresses:

FGT # diagnose sys sdwan internet-service-app-ctrl-list

Gmail(15817 4294836957): 64.233.191.19 6 443 Thu Apr 22 10:10:34 2021

Gmail(15817 4294836957): 142.250.128.83 6 443 Thu Apr 22 10:06:47 2021

Facebook(15832 4294836806): 69.171.250.35 6 443 Thu Apr 22 10:12:00 2021

Amazon(16492 4294836342): 3.226.60.231 6 443 Thu Apr 22 10:10:57 2021

Amazon(16492 4294836342): 52.46.135.211 6 443 Thu Apr 22 10:10:58 2021

Amazon(16492 4294836342): 52.46.141.85 6 443 Thu Apr 22 10:10:58 2021

Amazon(16492 4294836342): 52.46.155.13 6 443 Thu Apr 22 10:10:58 2021

Amazon(16492 4294836342): 54.82.242.32 6 443 Thu Apr 22 10:10:59 2021

YouTube(31077 4294838537): 74.125.202.138 6 443 Thu Apr 22 10:06:51 2021

YouTube(31077 4294838537): 108.177.121.119 6 443 Thu Apr 22 10:08:24 2021

YouTube(31077 4294838537): 142.250.136.119 6 443 Thu Apr 22 10:02:02 2021

YouTube(31077 4294838537): 142.250.136.132 6 443 Thu Apr 22 10:08:16 2021

YouTube(31077 4294838537): 142.250.148.100 6 443 Thu Apr 22 10:07:28 2021

YouTube(31077 4294838537): 142.250.148.132 6 443 Thu Apr 22 10:10:32 2021

YouTube(31077 4294838537): 172.253.119.91 6 443 Thu Apr 22 10:02:01 2021

YouTube(31077 4294838537): 184.150.64.211 6 443 Thu Apr 22 10:04:36 2021

YouTube(31077 4294838537): 184.150.168.175 6 443 Thu Apr 22 10:02:26 2021

YouTube(31077 4294838537): 184.150.168.211 6 443 Thu Apr 22 10:02:26 2021

YouTube(31077 4294838537): 184.150.186.141 6 443 Thu Apr 22 10:02:26 2021

YouTube(31077 4294838537): 209.85.145.190 6 443 Thu Apr 22 10:10:36 2021

YouTube(31077 4294838537): 209.85.200.132 6 443 Thu Apr 22 10:02:03 2021

To check the dynamic tunnel status:

diagnose sys link-monitor interface <name> <name>_0

For example:

diagnose sys link-monitor interface vd2-2

Interface(vd2-2): state(up, since Tue Jun 15 12:31:28 2021), bandwidth(up:1299bps, down:0bps), session count(IPv4:2, IPv6:0), tx(2409919 bytes), rx(5292290 bytes), latency(0.03), jitter(0.00), packet-loss(0.00).

diagnose sys link-monitor interface vd2-2 vd2-2_0

Interface(vd2-2_0): state(up, since Tue Jun 15 15:21:52 2021), bandwidth(up:640bps, down:0bps), session count(IPv4:0, IPv6:0), tx(102242 bytes), rx(16388 bytes), latency(0.03), jitter(0.00), packet-loss(0.00).

To check BGP learned routes and determine if they are used in SD-WAN service:

FGT # get router info bgp network 10.100.11.0/24

VRF 0 BGP routing table entry for 10.100.11.0/24

Paths: (2 available, best #2, table Default-IP-Routing-Table)

 Advertised to non peer-group peers:

  10.100.1.1

 Original VRF 0

 20 10

  10.100.1.1 from 10.100.1.1 (5.5.5.5)

  Origin incomplete metric 0, route tag 15, localpref 100, valid, external, best

   Community: 30:5

   Advertised Path ID: 2

   Last update: Thu Apr 22 10:27:27 2021

 Original VRF 0

 20 10

  10.100.1.5 from 10.100.1.5 (6.6.6.6)

  Origin incomplete metric 0, route tag 15, localpref 100, valid, external, best

   Community: 30:5

   Advertised Path ID: 1

   Last update: Thu Apr 22 10:25:50 2021

FGT # diagnose sys sdwan route-tag-list

Route-tag: 15, address: v4(1), v6(0)Last write/now: 6543391 6566007

    service(1), last read route-tag 15 at 6543420

Prefix(24): Address list(1):

    10.100.11.0-10.100.11.255 oif: 50 48

FGT # diagnose firewall proute list

list route policy info(vf=root):

id=2133196801(0x7f260001)   vwl_service=1(DataCenter)
vwl_mbr_seq=1 2 dscp_tag=0xff 0xff flags=0x40 order-addr tos=0x00

tos_mask=0x00   protocol=0   sport=0-65535   iif=0   dport=1-65535
oif=48(R150) oif=50(R160)

destination(1): 10.100.11.0-10.100.11.255

source wildcard(1): 0.0.0.0/0.0.0.0

hit_count=0 last_used=2021-04-22 10:25:10

SD-WAN bandwidth monitoring service

The bandwidth measuring tool is used to detect true upload and download speeds. Bandwidth tests can be run on demand or automated using a script, and can be useful when configuring SD-WAN SLA and rules to balance SD-WAN traffic.

The speed test tool requires a valid SD-WAN Bandwidth Monitoring Service license.

The speed test tool is compatible with iperf3.6 with SSL support. It can test the upload bandwidth to the FortiGate Cloud speed test service. It can initiate the server connection and send download requests to the server. The tool can be run up to 10 times a day .

FortiGate downloads the speed test server list. The list expires after 24 hours. One of the speed test servers is selected, based on user input. The speed test runs, testing upload and download speeds. The test results are shown in the command terminal.

To download the speed test server list:

\# execute speed-test-server download

Download completed.

To check the speed test server list:

\# execute speed-test-server list

AWS_West valid

     Host: 34.210.67.183 5204 fortinet

     Host: 34.210.67.183 5205 fortinet

     Host: 34.210.67.183 5206 fortinet

     Host: 34.210.67.183 5207 fortinet

Google_West valid

     Host: 35.197.55.210 5204 fortinet

     Host: 35.197.55.210 5205 fortinet

     Host: 35.197.55.210 5206 fortinet

     Host: 35.197.55.210 5207 fortinet

     Host: 35.230.2.124 5204 fortinet

     Host: 35.230.2.124 5205 fortinet

     Host: 35.230.2.124 5206 fortinet

Host: 35.230.2.124 5207 fortinet

Host: 35.197.18.234 5204 fortinet

Host: 35.197.18.234 5205 fortinet

Host: 35.197.18.234 5206 fortinet

Host: 35.197.18.234 5207 fortinet

To run the speed test:

You can run the speed test without specifying a server. The system will automatically choose one server from the list and run the speed test.

execute speed-test auto

The license is valid to run speed test.

Speed test quota for 2/1 is 9

current vdom=root

Run in uploading mode.

Connecting to host 35.230.2.124, port 5206

[16] local 172.16.78.185 port 2475 connected to 35.230.2.124 port 5206

[ID] Interval Transfer Bitrate Retr Cwnd

[16] 0.00-1.01 sec 11.0 MBytes 91.4 Mbits/sec 0 486 KBytes

[16] 1.01-2.00 sec 11.6 MBytes 98.4 Mbits/sec 0 790 KBytes

[16] 2.00-3.01 sec 11.0 MBytes 91.6 Mbits/sec 15 543 KBytes

[16] 3.01-4.01 sec 11.2 MBytes 94.2 Mbits/sec 1 421 KBytes

[16] 4.01-5.01 sec 11.2 MBytes 93.5 Mbits/sec 0 461 KBytes

- -

[ID] Interval Transfer Bitrate Retr

[16] 0.00-5.01 sec 56.1 MBytes 93.8 Mbits/sec 16 sender

[16] 0.00-5.06 sec 55.8 MBytes 92.6 Mbits/sec receiver

speed test Done.

Run in reverse downloading mode!

Connecting to host 35.230.2.124, port 5206

Reverse mode, remote host 35.230.2.124 is sending

[16] local 172.16.78.185 port 2477 connected to 35.230.2.124 port 5206

[ID] Interval Transfer Bitrate

[16] 0.00-1.00 sec 10.9 MBytes 91.4 Mbits/sec

[16] 1.00-2.00 sec 11.2 MBytes 93.9 Mbits/sec

[16] 2.00-3.00 sec 11.2 MBytes 94.0 Mbits/sec

[16] 3.00-4.00 sec 11.2 MBytes 93.9 Mbits/sec

[16] 4.00-5.00 sec 10.9 MBytes 91.1 Mbits/sec

- -

[ID] Interval Transfer Bitrate Retr

[16] 0.00-5.03 sec 57.5 MBytes 95.9 Mbits/sec 40 sender

[16] 0.00-5.00 sec 55.4 MBytes 92.9 Mbits/sec receiver

speed test Done

To run the speed test on a server farm or data center:

execute speed-test auto AWS_West

The license is valid to run speed test.

Speed test quota for 2/1 is 8

current vdom=root

Run in uploading mode.

Connecting to host 34.210.67.183, port 5205

To run the speed test on a local interface when there are multiple valid routes:

execute speed-test port1 Google_West

The license is valid to run speed test.

Speed test quota for 2/1 is 6

bind to local ip 172.16.78.202

current vdom=root

Specified interface port1 does not comply with default outgoing interface port2 in routing table!

Force to use the specified interface!

Run in uploading mode.

Connecting to host 35.197.18.234, port 5205

[11] local 172.16.78.202 port 20852 connected to 35.197.18.234 port 5205

[ID] Interval Transfer Bitrate Retr Cwnd

[11] 0.00-1.01 sec 10.7 MBytes 89.0 Mbits/sec 0 392 KBytes

[11] 1.01-2.01 sec 10.5 MBytes 88.5 Mbits/sec 1 379 KBytes

[11] 2.01-3.01 sec 11.3 MBytes 94.5 Mbits/sec 0 437 KBytes

[11] 3.01-4.01 sec 11.2 MBytes 94.3 Mbits/sec 0 478 KBytes

[11] 4.01-5.00 sec 11.3 MBytes 95.2 Mbits/sec 0 503 KBytes

- -

[ID] Interval Transfer Bitrate Retr

[11] 0.00-5.00 sec 55.1 MBytes 92.3 Mbits/sec 1 sender

[11] 0.00-5.04 sec 54.5 MBytes 90.7 Mbits/sec receiver

speed test Done.

Run in reverse downloading mode!

Connecting to host 35.197.18.234, port 5205

Reverse mode, remote host 35.197.18.234 is sending

[11] local 172.16.78.202 port 20853 connected to 35.197.18.234 port 5205

[ID] Interval Transfer Bitrate

[11] 0.00-1.00 sec 10.9 MBytes 91.1 Mbits/sec

[11] 1.00-2.00 sec 11.2 MBytes 94.0 Mbits/sec

[11] 2.00-3.00 sec 11.2 MBytes 94.0 Mbits/sec

[11] 3.00-4.00 sec 11.2 MBytes 94.0 Mbits/sec

[11] 4.00-5.00 sec 11.2 MBytes 94.0 Mbits/sec

- -

[ID] Interval Transfer Bitrate Retr

[11] 0.00-5.03 sec 57.4 MBytes 95.8 Mbits/sec 33 sender

[11] 0.00-5.00 sec 55.7 MBytes 93.4 Mbits/sec receiver

speed test Done.

To add a script to run a speed test automatically once every 24 hours:

```
config system auto-script
    edit "speedtest"
        set interval 86400
        set repeat 0
        set start auto
        set script "
execute speed-test-server download
execute speed-test"
    next
end
```

To view the results of the speed test script:

```
execute auto-script result speedtest
```

Using SNMP to monitor health check

You can monitor SD-WAN health check related statistics using SNMP. The MIB file can be downloaded by going to System > SNMP and clicking Download FortiGate MIB File.

The following OIDs can be monitored:

Name	OID	Description
fgVWLHealthCheckLink Number	.1.3.6.1.4.1.12356.10 1.4.9.1	The number of health check links in fgVWLHealthChec kLinkTable
fgVWLHealthCheckLink Table	.1.3.6.1.4.1.12356.10 1.4.9.2	SD-WAN health check statistics table. This table has a dependent expansion relationship with fgVdTable.Only health checks with a configured member link are present in this table.
fgVWLHealthCheckLink TableEntry	.1.3.6.1.4.1.12356.10 1.4.9.2.1	SD-WAN health check statistics on a virtual domain.
fgVWLHealthCheckLinkI D	.1.3.6.1.4.1.12356.10 1.4.9.2.1.1	SD-WAN health check link ID. Only health checks with configured member link are present in this table. Virtual-wan-link health check link IDs are only unique within a

Name	OID	Description
		virtual domain.
fgVWLHealthCheckLink Name	.1.3.6.1.4.1.12356.10 1.4.9.2.1.2	Health check name.
fgVWLHealthCheckLink Seq	.1.3.6.1.4.1.12356.10 1.4.9.2.1.3	SD-WAN member link sequence.
fgVWLHealthCheckLink State	.1.3.6.1.4.1.12356.10 1.4.9.2.1.4	Health check state on a specific member link.
fgVWLHealthCheckLink Latency	.1.3.6.1.4.1.12356.10 1.4.9.2.1.5	The average latency of a health check on a specific member link within last 30 probes, in float number.
fgVWLHealthCheckLink Jitter	.1.3.6.1.4.1.12356.10 1.4.9.2.1.6	The average jitter of a health check on a specific member link within last 30 probes, in float number.
fgVWLHealthCheckLink PacketSend	.1.3.6.1.4.1.12356.10 1.4.9.2.1.7	The total number of packets sent by a health check on a specific member link.
fgVWLHealthCheckLink PacketRecv	.1.3.6.1.4.1.12356.10 1.4.9.2.1.8	The total number of packets received by a health check on a specific member link.
fgVWLHealthCheckLink PacketLoss	.1.3.6.1.4.1.12356.10 1.4.9.2.1.9	The packet loss percentage of a health check on a

Name	OID	Description
		specific member link within last 30 probes, in float number.
fgVWLHealthCheckLink Vdom	.1.3.6.1.4.1.12356.10 1.4.9.2.1.10	The VDOM that the link monitor entry exists in.
		This name corresponds to the fgVdEntName used in fgVdTable.
fgVWLHealthCheckLink BandwidthIn	.1.3.6.1.4.1.12356.10 1.4.9.2.1.11	The available bandwidth of incoming traffic detected by a health check on a specific member link, in Mbps,
fgVWLHealthCheckLink BandwidthOut	.1.3.6.1.4.1.12356.10 1.4.9.2.1.12	The available bandwidth of outgoing traffic detected by a health check on a specific member link, in Mbps.
fgVWLHealthCheckLink BandwidthBi	.1.3.6.1.4.1.12356.10 1.4.9.2.1.13	The available bandwidth of bi-direction traffic detected by a health check on a specific member link, in Mbps.
fgVWLHealthCheckLinkI fName	.1.3.6.1.4.1.12356.10 1.4.9.2.1.14	SD-WAN member interface name.

Example

This example shows a SD-WAN health check configuration and its collected statistics.

To configure the SD-WAN health check:

```
config system sdwan
    set status enable
    config zone
        edit "virtual-wan-link"
        next
    end
    config members
        edit 1
            set interface "port1"
            set gateway 192.168.2.1
        next
        edit 2
            set interface "MPLS"
            set zone "SD-Zone2"
            set cost 20
        next
        edit 3
            set interface "port2"
        next
    end
    config health-check
        edit "pingserver"
            set server "8.8.8.8"
            set sla-fail-log-period 10
            set sla-pass-log-period 20
            set members 2 1 3
            config sla
```

```
        edit 1
            set link-cost-factor jitter packet-loss
            set packetloss-threshold 2
        next
      end
    next
  end
end
```

The collected statistics:

fgVWLHealthCheckLi nkID	.1.3.6.1.4.1.12356. 101.4.9.2.1.1	1	2	3
fgVWLHealthCheckLi nkName	.1.3.6.1.4.1.12356. 101.4.9.2.1.2	pings erver	pings erver	pings erver
fgVWLHealthCheckLi nkSeq	.1.3.6.1.4.1.12356. 101.4.9.2.1.3	2	1	3
fgVWLHealthCheckLi nkState	.1.3.6.1.4.1.12356. 101.4.9.2.1.4	0	0	0
fgVWLHealthCheckLi nkLatency	.1.3.6.1.4.1.12356. 101.4.9.2.1.5	39.30 2	43.12 4	44.34 8
fgVWLHealthCheckLi nkJitter	.1.3.6.1.4.1.12356. 101.4.9.2.1.6	4.346	3.951	5.05
fgVWLHealthCheckLi nkPacketSend	.1.3.6.1.4.1.12356. 101.4.9.2.1.7	3657 689	3657 689	3657 689
fgVWLHealthCheckLi nkPacketRecv	.1.3.6.1.4.1.12356. 101.4.9.2.1.8	31962 58	3220 258	32194 66
fgVWLHealthCheckLi nkPacketLoss	.1.3.6.1.4.1.12356. 101.4.9.2.1.9	0	0	0
fgVWLHealthCheckLi nkVdom	.1.3.6.1.4.1.12356. 101.4.9.2.1.10	root	root	root
fgVWLHealthCheckLi	.1.3.6.1.4.1.12356.	9999	9999	9999

nkBandwıdthIn	101.4.9.2.1.11	963	937	999
fgVWLHealthCheckLı	.1.3.6.1.4.1.12356.	9999	9999	9999
nkBandwıdthOut	101.4.9.2.1.12	981	953	998
fgVWLHealthCheckLı	.1.3.6.1.4.1.12356.	1999	1999	1999
nkBandwıdthBı	101.4.9.2.1.13	9944	9890	9997
fgVWLHealthCheckLı	.1.3.6.1.4.1.12356.	MPLS	port1	port2
nkIfName	101.4.9.2.1.14